D1200415

WITHDRAWN
FROM THE RECORDS OF THE
MID-CONTINENT PUBLIC LIBRARY

747 H279
Hastie, Jenny.
The interior design bible

MID-CONTINENT PUBLIC LIBRARY
Liberty Branch
1000 Kent Street
Liberty, MO 64068

LI

THE **INTERIOR DESIGN**
BIBLE

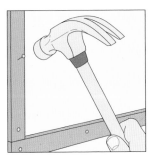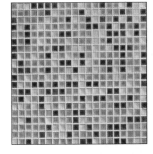

hamlyn

THE INTERIOR DESIGN
BIBLE

JENNY HASTIE

Idealhome

MID-CONTINENT PUBLIC LIBRARY
Liberty Branch
1000 Kent Street
Liberty, MO 64068

LI

MID-CONTINENT PUBLIC LIBRARY - QU

3 0003 00476157 1

An Hachette Livre UK Company
www.hachettelivre.co.uk

First published in Great Britain in 2009 by
Hamlyn, a division of Octopus Publishing
Group Ltd
2–4 Heron Quays, London E14 4JP
www.octopusbooks.co.uk

Design and layout © Octopus Publishing
Group Ltd 2009
Text © Octopus Publishing Group Ltd 2009
Photography © IPC Media Limited 2009

Distributed in the U.S. and Canada by
Octopus Books USA:
c/o Hachette Book Group USA
237 Park Avenue
New York NY 10017

All rights reserved. No part of this work
may be reproduced or utilized in any form
or by any means, electronic or mechanical,
including photocopying, recording or by
any information storage and retrieval
system, without the prior written permission
of the publisher.

ISBN 978-0-600-61725-9

A CIP catalogue record for this book is
available from the British Library

Printed and bound in China

10 9 8 7 6 5 4 3 2 1

CONTENTS

INTRODUCTION

Decorating the interior of your home helps bring the space to life. Selecting fabrics, colours and furniture and combining them to create unique room schemes is a process that should be a joy to undertake and one which leads to a home that's as individual as you are.

This book aims to demystify the process of interior design. For a thorough overview, you may choose to read it cover to cover, but equally you can dip in and out to find help with your current decorating decision, whether that's choosing a particular look and picking from the vast array of materials on the market, devising a way to make your space work harder for you, or mixing and matching accessories that will pull the whole scheme together.

Use the beautiful images to give you inspiration for your rooms, and follow your instincts as to which looks you like and which are practical for your lifestyle. If you approach the redesign of your home not only with careful planning but also a keen sense of enjoyment, you'll be well on your way to creating a home that's a pleasure for you to live in.

STYLE AND COLOUR

WHAT'S YOUR STYLE?

Each of us has our own personal style. Over the years, as we move from house to house, possibly acquiring partners, children and pets, our style alters as we change and grow but still remains unique to us.

While there will always be practical restraints on how we decorate – whether it is the amount of money we have to spend or necessary compromises with those with whom we live – the most successful decorating schemes are those which please our senses and suit our lifestyles. Influences from around the world, both historical and geographical, mean we're able to decorate in any style we wish. Antiques from Britain and France, textiles from India, Africa and China, and simple painted furniture from Scandinavia and The USA are all to be found within our homes. It's this exhilarating choice that can make picking one particular style seem an impossible feat. To make it easier, this introduction to styles is broken into three main strands:

traditional, classic and modern. You will find various ideas and combinations of styles within these three strands; when you've found a look you love, use the ideas as foundations for your own scheme at home.

While it's important you love the look of your rooms, you won't enjoy living in them unless the décor suits both your lifestyle and its surroundings. Aim to pick a style that works with the proportions of your home. Large pieces of contemporary furniture may crowd a tiny sitting room, while diminutive cottage-style antiques could look equally out of place in a modern open-plan apartment. Assess Your Space looks at how to get the most out of your available space, so if you'd like more inspiration turn to page 64.

Upholstery in delicate shades of soft oyster adds a luxurious feel to this sophisticated sitting room. Long linen curtains, which pool on the floor, look opulent and glamorous.

You could point to modern, traditional, classical and ethnic influences in this bedroom, but the unifying choice of colours and materials means they combine together successfully.

CHOOSING YOUR STYLE

Having a basic idea of your likes and dislikes will help you understand which style is right for you. Here are some questions to ask yourself.

Do you like informal or formal room layouts?

☐ Formal rooms have a symmetrical and organized furniture arrangement, frequently with sets of coordinating pieces of furniture. (Try a classic style)

☐ Informal rooms take a more relaxed approach to furniture layout: the furniture may not match, and the overall feeling is one of comfort. (Consider a traditional style)

Are you a traditionalist, or do you look to the future? Do you like:

☐ A historical look? (A traditional style may be for you)

☐ A look that's up to the minute? (A modern style may be the best option)

☐ A style that will stand the test of time? (A classic style may suit your rooms)

What kind of atmosphere do you like your rooms to have?

☐ Simple and restrained. (Try a classic or modern style)

☐ Cosy. (a traditional style may suit you best)

☐ Streamlined or organized. (Go for either a classic or modern style)

What kind of furniture instantly appeals to you?

☐ Sophisticated furniture made from top-quality materials. (Try a classic or modern style)

☐ Antique or vintage furniture that's been handed down the generations. (Try a traditional style)

☐ Classic designs that won't date. (Try a classic or modern style)

Remember: there's no right answer to any of these questions; the key is to be honest with yourself and choose a look that feels right for you.

TRADITIONAL STYLE

Traditional style is warm, cosy and expected. To create a room decorated in the traditional style it's important that the scheme looks as though it has evolved over time, so choose timeless ingredients and subtle (decorating) shades for the perfect traditional mix.

You can decorate according to a historical period, or in keeping with the age of your house if you live in a period property, but it's also possible to create a successful traditional style in a modern home simply by collecting together a well-chosen arrangement of pieces of furniture, accessories and decorative elements that are selected for their timeless, traditional qualities, their understated charm, and their weathered yet easy appeal. Well-loved pieces with vintage charm are preferable to anything that looks too new.

Choose natural materials, which take on more character as they age. Wood that burnishes when polished, stone that develops a rich patina, carpets and natural flooring that bring a mix of texture and pattern to rooms – all are materials which help create a style that looks as if it has developed over time. Fabrics for curtains, cushions, bedlinen and upholstery include chintz, linen, cotton prints, tweed and wool; whatever you choose, the emphasis is on fabrics that have a naturalness and soft drape.

When it comes to choosing furniture, go for antiques or pieces of modern furniture that have been designed to resemble designs from our past. Plain timber cabinetry such as wooden kitchen chairs, chests of drawers in bedrooms, and dressers in kitchens and dining rooms all conjure up a traditional air, while in the sitting room unstructured, loose covers on sofas and armchairs suit the style. Although the room's layout may look informal, the furniture is arranged carefully to fill the available space; traditional-style rooms contain plenty of furniture but are not overcrowded.

ASPECTS OF TRADITIONAL STYLE

Traditional style can be interpreted in many ways, but the most popular looks to recreate in today's homes are Traditional Country, Traditional Scandinavian and Traditional Beach House. Over the next few pages you will find ways to recreate these looks, and while each look is unique you will also see similarities between the styles – in the materials chosen, for example, or the atmosphere created by the finished room.

There's no need to follow a single style slavishly, and it's also possible to reinterpret the looks for your home by adding aspects of the classic and modern styles covered later in the chapter. So, if after looking at these styles you realize you love the country look, but prefer it with a modern twist, see Modern Country (page 30) for further inspiration. These two styles aren't too far apart in influence, but the modern execution is less rustic. Or, if you prefer a little glitz and glamour in your rooms, you can add a touch of Classic Glamour (see page 22) to any of these traditional looks by introducing some luxurious fabrics to the mix: exchange plain cotton bedspreads for a satin throw on a bed, or add some textured silk cushions to sofas or armchairs.

A selection of cushions and throws in a mix of natural, textural fabrics brings comfort and cosiness to this traditional living room, while mirrors and glass accessories help the daylight move around the room.

Floral curtains, plain painted walls and accessories in pastel tones of sage green and pale pink all combine to create a scheme with traditional country overtones. Pretty sheer drapes add a sense of romance.

Key characteristics

Materials: wood, stone, tiles, wool carpet, natural flooring.

Furniture: antique, upholstered, well-made wooden furniture, loose covers.

Fabrics: chintz, linen, cotton, prints, tweed, wool.

Patterns: florals, stripes, checks.

Influences and key words: historical, not bucking the trend, rough-hewn, weathered, timeless, loved, heirloom.

TRADITIONAL COUNTRY

Comfort is the byword here; there is nothing outrageous about this look. Inspired by the idealized interiors of traditional country cottages, materials are natural – think stone, wool, wood, cotton and linen – and the atmosphere is soothing and relaxing.

Create your room scheme by concentrating on paint, wallpapers and fabrics in soft, light colours that hark back to traditional shades yet sit well in today's interiors. Shades that are reminiscent of the natural colours of the countryside will help evoke the atmosphere whatever the age of your house: pale blue is the colour of summer skies in the country; soft yellows and apple and sage greens are extremely easy to live with and their gentle tones are soothing and comforting. A good place to start is to use these as background shades, for example by painting them on walls; this is not the place for eye-catching brights or garish wallpaper choices. Avoid shiny surfaces, too; this look is about waxed rather than varnished wood or laminates, chalky paints rather than satin finishes.

Furniture plays a key role in creating this look. You can choose cottage-style antiques or new pieces in traditional styles, but ensure the design of the furniture is neither too grand nor forbidding. The pieces need to look as though they can be used with ease every day, and in doing so they will age gracefully, becoming essential and much-loved items in your household. When choosing both furniture and accessories, avoid anything that makes the scheme look too coordinated by combining new pieces with vintage finds.

Your decorating scheme

Colours: choices are fresh and light pastel shades such as apple green, pale pink, primrose yellow, sky blue.

Fabrics: for windows, sheers, floral sheers, floral cottons; for soft furnishings, floral chintzes, plain cotton, linen, wool.

Flooring: downstairs, go for wood or tiles; upstairs, a tufted wool carpet adds texture and tactile softness.

Furniture: choose comfortable upholstery, simple plain timber and white- or cream-painted wood and metal pieces.

Get the look for less

Give a basic bedstead the romantic look of a traditional half-tester by fixing a simple wire coronet to the wall above the bed and hanging a pair of ready-made sheer curtains so they fall either side of the bedhead.

A sturdy wooden table and chairs are all that's needed to furnish a traditional country-style dining room. Here a wood-burning stove and rough timber fire surround add to the room's traditional charm.

KEY STYLE FEATURES

Crisp apple-green walls are calm, fresh and a perfect starting point for bringing traditional country style to a bedroom.

Simple white-painted curtain tie-backs are a traditional and practical detail.

Painted wooden furniture is a key look for traditional country-style bedrooms.

A wrought-iron bedstead, painted cream, suits the country style perfectly.

TRADITIONAL SCANDINAVIAN

The fresh looks and clear colours of Scandinavian style make it a popular choice in today's homes, as the colour palette ensures rooms are light and airy, while the furniture is comfortable and appealing, and looks good in homes of any age.

style and colour

White was traditionally chosen by Scandinavians to maximize the amount of natural light in their northern homes, and the colour choices for this traditional style are based on a limited colour palette. Luckily this makes choosing colours reasonably straightforward: begin with a background of white or off-white, then add colour with splashes of cool blue, warming cherry red or deep forest green. If pure white seems too cold, go for a warmer shade such as pale cream or rich ivory.

Flooring is pale in colour and also helps reflect light around the room. If you'd like to lay carpet, choose white or cream wool, and in kitchens or dining rooms go for pale timbers such as birch or beech wood. To faithfully recreate the look of traditional Scandinavian rooms you may like to invest in Gustavian-style carved wooden furniture that was originally produced in the eighteenth century: you will find both reproduction and antique pieces are available. However, simple pieces of modern white-painted wooden furniture will conjure up the mood of this style just as effectively. Fabrics and soft furnishings are restrained yet elegant; linens and cottons in simple traditional patterns such as checks and ginghams are ideal, chosen in two-tone shades of cream and red or white and blue to bring colour and pattern to the otherwise neutral room scheme.

Your decorating scheme

Colours: white is key, while shades include deep and pale blues, fir greens and warm reds.
Fabrics: linens and cottons in checks, plains and delicate sprigged florals.
Flooring: pure wool carpets in cream or off-white, plus pale timber flooring such as birch or beech.
Furniture: carved wooden furniture reminiscent of the eighteenth-century Gustavian period, or simpler painted wooden pieces. Sofas and armchairs are upholstered in plain or checked fabrics in a traditional colourway.

This Scandinavian-inspired dining room is filled with painted wooden furniture. Accents of duck-egg blue, a traditional Scandinavian decorating shade, inject some muted colour to the sophisticated ivory and gold room scheme. Shimmering glass – both on the table and in the chandelier – brings warmth and sparkle to the room.

KEY STYLE FEATURES

Traditional Scandinavian décor lends a calm and relaxing air to this sitting room.

The display of delicate blue and white china plates is a traditional touch.

White-painted wooden furniture is a key feature of this style.

The traditionally shaped sofas have elegantly carved legs. A mix of blue and white patterned cushions adds extra pattern.

An accent wall hung with pale blue and white floral wallpaper brings pattern and subtle colour to the room.

TRADITIONAL BEACH HOUSE

Capture the spirit of seaside living with this style. Cool blues mixed with vintage furnishings and reclaimed wooden floorboards are easy to live with, and the laid-back look brings a holiday feel to everyday homes, even if you live miles from the beach.

This is the perfect style for people who like their rooms to look well-loved, with furniture that's been used by many for years and a décor that's fresh, light and easy to achieve. There's nothing grand or imposing about this style; instead the rooms have a welcoming, relaxed appeal in keeping with homes remembered from much-enjoyed holidays by the seaside.

The look is pared down and practical: on the floor, wooden boards are a natural choice and are easy to keep clean, while over-long sheer curtains in natural fabrics such as cotton and linen frame any window beautifully and let the sunshine flood in whatever the time of year.

Accent colours can be either bold or muted, depending on the look and the atmosphere you'd like to create, but whichever you choose white is usually the main background colour. Mix white, bright blue and splashes of strong scarlet for a look that nods towards the colours in traditional Greek fishing villages; or go for atmospheric soft greys, warm creams and pale beiges for a beach-house interpretation of today's popular neutral palettes.

Your decorating scheme

Colours: inspired by nature and the hues of seascapes – deep and pale blues, muted greens, white and beige neutrals. Add vibrancy with splashes of bright blue or red.
Fabrics: natural unbleached cotton and linens, striped ticking.
Flooring: keep floors simple – natural or white-painted wooden flooring looks best.
Furniture: mix and match painted and plain wooden pieces for vintage beach-house appeal; loose covers made from cotton or linen, in white or pale shades, are perfect for sofas.

Get the look for less

Loose white covers on a sofa are ideal for creating a sitting room with relaxed beach-house style, but they aren't the most practical choice. Opt for sofas with washable covers, or buy an extra set; both options will prolong the life and looks of the sofas.

The walls in this airy sitting room are painted a fresh blue, while the curtains are simple and sheer. Loose covers on sofas lend an informal air, and are easy to remove and clean.

KEY STYLE FEATURES

Muted colours, a wooden floor and painted timber furniture bring seaside style to this dining room.

Simple fisherman's-style lamps add a nautical touch.

A dresser is a traditional piece of furniture and ideal for this style. It's a practical choice too, keeping dining essentials close to hand.

Striped chair cushions in shades of white, pale blue and sand pretty up the simple chairs.

CLASSIC STYLE

Classic styles are harmonious, elegant and designed to last. A sense of control and order is evident when you enter the room, and it's clear that the design and layout have been thoroughly planned.

One of the key words of classic style is symmetry. The formal nature of a symmetrical arrangement lends an air of classic restraint to a room. Think of a pair of sofas set opposite one another on either side of a fireplace, a dining table encircled by a set of matching chairs, or a pair of terracotta planters arranged either side of a front door. This simple act of balancing one item with a matching other lends a particular aura of calmness and order to even the most simple arrangements. It's also easy for even a novice decorator to achieve.

CREATE THE LOOK

As with traditional style, the materials chosen play a large part in creating the overall look of the room. Furniture and furnishings should be of high quality and chosen with care, so that they work well with each other and with the proportions of the room. Mirrored glass is a perennial favourite – think of Venetian looking

glasses together with mirrored furniture and accessories and you will envisage a room with a definite air of luxury. Top-quality hardwoods also lend the appearance of glamour and expensiveness to a room's completed look, so consider choosing exotic hardwood floors or beautifully crafted antique walnut or mahogany furniture. Avoid anything that looks too rough and ready: quality and elegance is key.

A classic look is timeless, so furniture should be simple and unfussy in design, in shapes which won't date. Whether you've got the budget to collect antiques or prefer new furniture, go for streamlined, unadorned pieces that will look good in the room in years to come. Well-made upholstery with fitted, rather than loose, covers is one option; if you prefer a more contemporary look, choose design classics from twentieth- and twenty-first-century furniture designers which you will love to keep in your home for ever.

Iridescent wallpaper brings a pearly shimmer to this bedroom, and the crisp bedlinen has a subtle metallic thread. Layering bedlinen and blankets adds a touch of hotel luxury.

ASPECTS OF CLASSIC STYLE

The following pages show just three ways in which classic style might be interpreted: Classic Glamour, Classic Contemporary and Classic Comfort. Each has its own characteristics, but they all share a stylishness and symmetry, and attention to quality.

You can broaden the possibilities further by incorporating traditional or modern elements, to make the style your own. You could make Classic Contemporary more cutting-edge, for example, by choosing modern pieces of furniture while still maintaining the ordered room layout of classic style. Classic Comfort and Traditional Country have many similarities; the classic version is simply less rustic and more formal. Move between styles by adding or subtracting elements depending on the look you'd like to achieve: for a rustic look, add furniture with antique finishes, or choose sprigged floral patterns on fabrics or wallpaper; for a more classic look, go for soft cream carpet, deep-pile rugs and quality upholstery. Whichever you choose, aim to use design elements that appeal to you and coordinate with each other.

If you love the look of classic but contemporary, then think about the classic pairing of black and white. Keep white as the main colour, and add drama with accents of black.

Key characteristics

Materials: glass, mirror, hardwoods, top-quality materials, crystal, carpet.
Furniture: Art Deco, design classics, quality antiques, tailored upholstery.
Fabrics: silk, velvet, linens, luxurious fabrics.
Patterns: ornate florals, substantial stripes.
Influences and key words: symmetry, formal, monochrome, pure colours, simple lines, lack of clutter, good-looking, well-made, elegant.

CLASSIC GLAMOUR

Luxurious materials help create rooms with a sense of elegance and opulence. They not only look wonderful but feel good to touch, so they appeal to our sensuous natures, encouraging us to relax and feel extra-special.

Glamour demands that all the materials you choose are sumptuous, both to look at and to feel, whether by hand or underfoot. Go for curtains made from shimmering fabrics such as silk and satins, and ensure carpet has a thick pile and feels soft and luxurious to walk on. Keep colours muted: a soft and neutral palette of pinks, taupe, mushroom and creams looks comforting yet glamorous. For the height of elegance opt for ice blues mixed with white and splashes of shimmering silver.

Accessories come into their own with this style and are a great way of adding glamorous touches to a room that has been decorated on a tight budget. Simple bedsteads and sofas can be turned into opulent pieces by piling them high with throws and cushions chosen in iridescent silks, satin velvets or *faux* furs. Hang beautifully framed mirrors on the wall, and place mirrored accessories such as picture frames or lamp bases around the room; the glass looks luxurious and its reflective properties bring a touch of extra sparkle to the room.

Your decorating scheme

Colours: frosty, muted and pastel, such as pink and ice blue, with accents of gold and silver.
Fabrics: glossy and luxurious – silks and satins predominate, plus *faux* furs for tactile softness.
Flooring: carpet, preferably deep pile and creamy in shade, or rich dark wooden boards.
Furniture: mix classic upholstery with mirrored or oriental pieces.

Get the look for less

The glamorous look is one that's clutter-free, so ensure you've plenty of storage to hide your essentials from view. Instead of buying an expensive blanket box or chest of drawers, group a collection of lidded baskets together at the end of the bed for a practical yet sophisticated storage solution for blankets or shoes.

A highly decorative wallpaper provides an ornate backdrop for this classic living room, while the ice-blue and cream colour scheme is understated yet luxurious. The formal layout and sophisticated furnishings create a look that demands to be noticed.

KEY STYLE FEATURES

The sophisticated colour scheme of this inviting bedroom shows that glamorous doesn't have to mean glitzy.

The all-important symmetry is here, in keeping with the classic style.

Finishing touches can make all the difference; a vase of garden flowers would be pretty, but this orchid provides just the right note of elegance.

A large imitation-fur throw adds instant tactile glamour.

CLASSIC CONTEMPORARY

This mix of traditional and contemporary elements creates a look that's very now and yet won't date. Here you have the opportunity to add modern pieces of design to a classic layout, creating a space that's eye-catching, welcoming and relaxing.

To achieve the look, you need to avoid anything that's too fashionable – it will soon be out of fashion and so won't be deemed to have classic style. Instead, look for well-made pieces of furniture with simple shapes and sophisticated lines, or contemporary designs that have been winning plaudits since they were launched. Sofas and armchairs should have fitted rather than loose covers, so their clean lines can be appreciated. Arranging the furniture in a symmetrical or traditional layout helps the room look ageless even if the furniture is modern in design. Ensure there's plenty of space within the room: don't cram it with unnecessary pieces of occasional furniture.

Colour and pattern choices need to be restrained and elegant, ensuring they too will not date. If you love geometric designs, go for modern patterns with simple squares, stripes, circles or checks on luxurious fabrics that also feel good to touch, such as chenille or velvet. Keep to a sophisticated yet simple colour palette: striking monochrome black and white is a good choice, or for a gentler mix try a selection of muted modern neutrals such as beiges, pinks and taupe. Use accessories to bring a more contemporary note to the room: citrus-bright cushions on the sofa, for example.

Your decorating scheme

Colours: classic colour combinations such as black and white, or restrained neutrals such as warm pinks, creams and off-whites.
Fabrics: good-quality linens, cottons and leather.
Flooring: cream or off-white carpet.
Furniture: simple shapes with a contemporary twist, although avoid any pieces that are too stark or ultra-modern.

Get the look for less

Instead of investing in brand-new armchairs, consider whether your existing ones can be updated. Re-upholstering tired armchairs in a modern fabric is a clever designer's trick that gives a new lease of life to old furniture.

The symmetrical layout of the room, the styling of the sofas and armchair and the console tables holding pairs of lamps are all classic elements, but the bold modern stripes and the zingy lime give the room a contemporary appeal.

KEY STYLE FEATURES

A clever mix of furniture and a muted palette ensure this room has classic charm with a modern twist.

The mirrored console table is a modern take on a classic piece of furniture.

The cream leather ottoman is chic and modern in style.

A traditional cream sofa provides the focal point for the room.

Silk scatter cushions add a luxurious touch.

CLASSIC COMFORT

If you love a comfortable country style, with wooden furniture and traditional upholstery, but prefer your furniture to have an air of good quality and to be new rather than antique, then this may be the look for you.

Classic Comfort has its roots in Traditional Country (see page 14), but there's nothing rough-hewn about this look. Furniture is well made from quality wood, and upholstery is plump and welcoming.

To avoid the room becoming too cottagey, avoid busy patterns for both wallpapers and fabrics. Instead, go for a mix of plain and mid-sized patterns that will add enough interest without the room looking fussy or heavily detailed. Decorate in blocks of solid colour, picking paint colours and fabrics in traditional country shades such as sky blue, dusky pink and soft yellow. The tones of the colours are important: avoid any

shade which looks too insipid or the room will look washed out and without vibrancy. You're aiming for a timeless look which creates a relaxing mood.

When choosing furniture, go for solid timber pieces with a natural finish, rather than anything that is too heavily carved or ornate. Sofas and armchairs should be inviting places for a chat with friends or to curl up with a book: plain white or cream linen and cotton loose covers, or well-made fitted covers, are both good options for upholstery; they maximize the welcome factor as well as adding a stylish look to the room. Add cushions for extra comfort and pattern.

Your decorating scheme

Colours: traditional country shades such as sky blue, dusky pink and soft yellow.
Fabrics: plain upholstery, mid-sized florals (avoid country-cottage sprigs).
Flooring: neutral-coloured or plain wool carpet with a deep pile or a textured finish.
Furniture: best possible quality wooden furniture and upholstery with chunky, simple shapes and little carving.

Add a touch of comfort in the bedroom by including a classically styled armchair. Curtains and accessories in a rosy pink suit the room's cottagey air, but the cream carpet is soft and luxurious, a more classic touch.

KEY STYLE FEATURES

A yellow and white colour scheme is a classic choice – fresh and welcoming without being too cottagey.

The sofa and armchair are traditional in shape, but there's nothing rustic about the crisp white upholstery.

Printed yellow and white curtains bring just enough pattern and colour to this sitting room.

A green throw looks cosy and adds a splash of contrasting colour to the limited decorative scheme.

MODERN STYLE

Modern style is up to date, taking the best of the decorating styles around today and paring them down so they work at home. Modern interpretations of favourite looks ensure that interior design will keep evolving, while new ideas challenge our design preconceptions.

When it comes to decorating a home, lovers of modern styles realize that they don't have to fill their homes with expensive cutting-edge design. Instead it's about assembling a room that works for today's lifestyles, distilling traditional or classic styles to get a look that's right for now yet easy to live with. Well-chosen furniture is given plenty of space, while displays of ornaments or artwork are simple and striking. Storage is streamlined and organized, and rooms are more aesthetically pleasing because of this.

Materials are a mix of natural and man-made, encompassing smooth leather upholstery, glass coffee tables and shelving units in living areas, to shimmering vinyl or colourful rubber floors in kitchens and bathrooms. Display is central to this look, whether you're using a bold patterned wallpaper to turn a wall into a talking point, or shelves to display a set of sculptural vases and ornaments.

Colours are clean; choose tones that are bright, fresh and clear, such as bold scarlet, sky blue or egg-yolk yellow to give your rooms a contemporary feel. If you don't know where to begin, a plain white background can be a good starting point, then use upholstery or bedlinen to add blocks of solid colour to the room.

ASPECTS OF MODERN STYLE

The variations of modern style recreated here are three of the most popular today: Modern Country, Modern Ethnic and Modern Coastal. You can pick and choose the aspects of each that please you most, and also incorporate more classic or traditional touches.

If you like ethnic pieces or patterns, but feel that recreating the entire Modern Ethnic look would not suit you, you could use a few ethnic-inspired accessories to give a room an instant lift; several cushions on a sofa in a Classic Comfort sitting room will add just enough eclecticism to liven it up. Alternatively, if you like the earthy colour scheme of Modern Ethnic style, but aren't partial to the accessories, then combine these rich colours with the simple furnishings of Modern Country to create a stylish room that's both warm and welcoming. Modern Coastal style is an update of Traditional Beach House; it also takes its inspiration from the sea, but there are fewer obvious references to the seaside, and the furniture has crisp, clean lines. Use ideas from both sections here to create a fusion of the two. If you'd love to add a bit of pizzazz to a modern décor, then take a leaf out of the Classic Glamour style and introduce some sumptuously tactile ingredients, such as deep-pile rugs or ultra-soft wool or *faux*-fur throws on beds and sofas, to bring sparkle and glitz to your rooms.

A modern sofa with bright red upholstery provides the focal point in this sitting room, and is combined with dark-stained bamboo furniture and delicate glass and china accessories to create a room that's filled with Eastern influences.

Key characteristics

Materials: metal, glass, wood, leather, laminate, quality vinyl flooring.

Furniture: simple shapes, contemporary pieces, collectors' items.

Fabrics: top-quality cotton, colourful fleece, finely woven wool.

Patterns: blocks of colour, geometric, large-scale.

Influences and key words: simple, up to date, restrained, streamlined, planned, airy, individual.

TOP Oak furniture and a cream decorating scheme ensure the room has plenty of country-style charm yet still looks up to date.

RIGHT The seascape painting above the fireplace has provided the basis for the room's décor. Simple wooden furniture and a well-dressed yet understated table setting mean the room has a calm yet welcoming atmosphere for a meal.

MODERN COUNTRY

Modern country is a pared-down version of Traditional Country (see page 14). As the furniture and furnishings are simpler and more up to date, this style is a practical choice for today's homes where space is often at a premium and shared with others.

(see page 14)

style and colour

Success with this style involves extrapolating the basic country look; the influences are similar but the overall look is less romantic and whimsical than its traditional cousin. There is wooden furniture, traditional patterns and an overall cosy feel, but with a modern slant. Instead of rustic timber flooring go for engineered boards or laminate flooring that looks as good as the real thing yet is more practical. Or, if you prefer to lay tiles, choose non-slip ceramic or pre-sealed terracotta rather than unsealed terracotta.

Choose emulsion paint for the walls in clear bright shades; avoid chalky finishes, which may look too traditional. Wooden furniture is perfect for this style but antiques may not be the solution for your lifestyle – look instead for dining tables and kitchen surfaces made from pale woods. Choose unfinished wood so the surfaces can be scrubbed down after use, or opt for a clear lacquered finish which lets the natural beauty of the wood shine through.

Let the sunshine pour into the rooms with sheer curtains or blinds; avoid dark, heavy drapes, which will look too traditional. White and cream fabrics, either plain or with a delicate, contemporary pattern, are an ideal choice.

Your decorating scheme

Colours: fresh, bright pastel or warm cream shades for walls and curtains.
Fabrics: plains, small prints. Avoid combining lots of patterns or your room will look too traditional.
Flooring: laminate wood flooring as a substitute for traditional floorboards, or tufted wool carpets.
Furniture: keep it simple, with modern timber pieces either stained or varnished to take advantage of the look of the natural wood.

Quick trick

A waxed cotton or PVC tablecloth is ideal for family dining rooms and helps protect your table's surface. Buying a length of fabric off the roll is an instant way to bring some colour and pattern into your kitchen/diner.

A patchwork quilt is the focal point for this bedroom. Keeping the walls and curtains plain and choosing simple wooden furniture means the room retains a calm, modern look.

KEY STYLE FEATURES

This family breakfast room reinterprets country style, achieving a traditional feel with modern colours and furniture.

Colourful printed cushions and a practical waxed cotton tablecloth bring real country style to the modern table and dining chairs.

Practical wooden laminate is a modern-day alternative to rustic wooden floorboards.

The white-painted cupboard, with the chest of drawers placed below, create a modern version of the traditional dresser.

MODERN ETHNIC

Modern Ethnic is a distillation of the ethnic look (now outdated), where rooms had a 'theme'. This style lends itself to rooms you'd like to be inviting and relaxed, but that incorporate eclectic touches to add a sense of the exotic.

To create this look at home you need get the right balance between ethnic and contemporary. It's also important to take one region or country as the basis for your room's decorative scheme, to prevent the finished room looking muddled. A good starting point is to go for an ethnic piece of furniture that makes a statement, such as a large and ornately carved wardrobe or dramatic four-poster bed, and let it take centre stage. You can balance this with smaller pieces of furniture sourced locally to avoid overkill. Then build up the look with a few well-chosen regional artefacts and decorative details, which can include a whole range of accessories from cushions, wall-hangings, rugs and throws to ornaments, sculpture and art. If you love collecting artefacts you can ensure your room will constantly evolve and change through the years as you add to your displays.

Colours are earthy and natural, with splashes of zingy brights to add vibrancy and liveliness to the scheme. Balance the colours with plenty of white or neutral-coloured walls and furnishings. Use fabrics to bring colour and pattern to the room; the bold and geometric patterns of ethnic soft furnishings often come in a range of delicious earthy and warm colourways. These can be made into curtains, cushion covers and throws, while rugs bring colour to neutral flooring.

Your decorating scheme

Colours: earthy, natural, with splashes of warm bright shades.
Fabrics: simple organic patterns, animal prints, handwoven textiles.
Flooring: natural flooring and dark-stained timber, topped with colourful or textured rugs.
Furniture: dark hardwood, or stained to resemble exotic woods such as teak. It may be carved, or look hand-made.

Insider info

If the furniture you're buying has been imported, check that it is made from wood taken from sustainable forests or made from recycled wood, such as reclaimed teak.

This home office demonstrates the appeal of Modern Ethnic. The décor is simple, in shades of taupe and chocolate, letting the colonial-style desk take centre stage.

KEY STYLE FEATURES

Choosing ethnic elements so they work within a modern setting results in a relaxed interpretation of ethnic style.

The modern cube storage unit displays an assortment of interesting artefacts, picked up on travels abroad.

A collection of cushions brings colour and pattern to the plain cream sofa.

The cream curtains with their simple brown border are understated and unfussy, and complement the colour scheme perfectly.

MODERN COASTAL

Inspired by seascapes and coastal walks, this is a bright, light style, recalling the natural materials and airy shades of the seaside. Rooms feel fresh and modern and are inviting places to be in whatever the age of the house.

Modern Coastal uses similar colours to Traditional Beach House (see page 18). However, while the traditional look is slightly rough and ready, you will need clean-lined furniture and blocks of colour to capture this style. For background shades, pick contemporary colours such as pale crisp blues, sandy neutrals or watery aqua. Then bring liveliness and vibrancy to the scheme with accents of brighter shades such as scarlets and turquoise. Keep window treatments light and airy; avoid heavy drapes and instead choose pale cotton or linen floor-length curtains, which can move in the breeze and let the sunshine flood in. Simple white roller or Roman blinds are another modern window treatment that is ideal for this look. Patterns should be up to date: go for geometric patterns and modern prints, avoiding florals and traditional motifs.

Underfoot, opt for sandy-toned natural flooring in a contemporary weave, plain wool carpets in off-white, or smooth wood or wood-effect flooring made from vinyl or laminate, depending on the room you are decorating. Furniture with simple, boxy shapes is ideal, and fitted upholstery covers, rather than loose, give sofas and armchairs a more modern silhouette; while occasional pieces such as wicker chairs and coffee tables also fit naturally into this relaxed, easy style. Modern artwork with references to the seaside will contribute to the finished look: be inspired to find decorating colours for the room among such prints.

Your decorating scheme

Colours: pale blues and sandy neutrals, accented with brights such as red and turquoise.
Fabrics: cotton in plains and contemporary prints.
Flooring: laminate, carpet, natural flooring.
Furniture: fitted upholstery covers, wicker, modern pieces.

A cool and calm colour palette evokes the shades of the seaside, with bursts of scarlet adding a sense of vibrancy and fun. Printed cotton curtains let the sunshine flood into the room.

KEY STYLE FEATURES

This modern living room is full of seaside touches without overdoing the theme.

A seaside motif underlines the coastal style.

The wicker chaise longue, with its thick-cushioned seat covered in sailcloth, speaks of summer and carefree outdoor living.

The strong aqua of the walls is picked up in the patterns of the cushions, keeping the colour scheme simple.

COLOUR AND PATTERN

Adding colour and pattern to your home is fun and is the starting point for any decorative room scheme. It's creative, subjective and your chance to express yourself and say 'This is my home, and I like it this way'.

Every decorative scheme is a mix of colours, patterns and textures. Each material used will provide an element of all three, but in most cases one or two will dominate and guide your choice. For example, floral fabric is chosen for its colour and pattern, while natural flooring has a neutral colour, a textured finish and a subtle pattern. To get your rooms looking just how you want them, it helps to understand how colours and patterns influence the look of the finished décor. The qualities of different materials and textures are then explored in detail in Finishes and Furniture, while if you'd like to understand the basis of a decorative scheme, turn to Your Design Scheme.

ABOVE Off-white and cream neutral shades help rooms appear spacious and light.

LEFT Blue is a calming colour choice for bedrooms, and its association with the elements water and air means it often creates a relaxing atmosphere.

USING COLOUR FOR MOOD

Every colour has its own mood and, while your own response to colours will be unique, there are some general attributes which apply to particular hues.

Red, orange and yellow are warm colours. They are eye-catching and stimulating, welcoming and rich. Ideal as accent colours, they can also be used to make rooms appear cosy as these colours seem to come towards you when you look at them.

Blue, violet and blue-greens are cool colours. Calming and space-enhancing, they seem to recede when painted on walls.

Green is naturally soothing and restful to look at. Mixed with blue it becomes cooler, while mixed with yellow it starts to look warmer.

Neutral shades bring a sense of space to colour schemes. Although these have traditionally been considered to be black, white and grey, nowadays we tend to think in terms of the natural shades of cream, stone and beige. These modern neutral shades coordinate well with both warm and cool colours.

While there are only a few pure colours there is an infinite variety of tones, and it is these colour tones that we mix and match to create our own individual decorative schemes. A dark tone is created by adding black to the pure colour, while a light tone is created by adding white to the pure colour.

Deep crimson walls warm up this contemporary sitting/dining room. The strong red walls are balanced by choosing white painted furniture and pale timber flooring, giving an overall impression of a modern, lively and colourful room.

COLOUR CHOICES FOR DIFFERENT ROOMS

You can use colour to help you create any atmosphere in your home, from calming to invigorating. Bear in mind how the room is used to help you decide which colours to choose.

Hallways should be welcoming and bright, and as people don't linger in a hall they can often take a stronger shade than a room that's used for relaxing. Bright citrus yellows, for example, are especially invigorating and can work extremely well in halls. If you have stairs in the hallway, you may need to continue the same colour up the stairwell and on the landing, so you should ensure the colour still appeals to you when it is applied to the upstairs walls as well.

Living rooms are for both relaxing and entertaining. Muted tones or neutral shades used as a background colour will help create a relaxing environment where you and your guests will feel comfortable. To bring some energy to the scheme you might introduce an accent wall covered in a brightly patterned wallpaper, or choose dramatic curtains and colourful accessories.

Kitchens are used throughout the day, so choose a background colour that's easy to live with and doesn't dominate this busy room.

Separate **dining rooms** are convivial places used solely for entertaining, and as they are often used in the evening they can be decorated with paints and wallpapers in darker, dramatic shades such as deep red or midnight blue which work well when illuminated by artificial lights.

Bedrooms are for sleeping and winding down. In adult rooms, soothing lilacs and pale blues aid restfulness and sleep. Children love bright colours but they may be too distracting: keep walls pale and add splashes of colour with accessories that can be easily changed as the child grows up.

Bathrooms are often decorated in watery shades, such as blues, whites and aquas; these are also relaxing colours, an aid to unwinding in the tub after a hectic day. Natural shades of beige and stone bring warmth to walls and are also a good choice for bathrooms and shower-rooms, helping to balance the cool white of sanitaryware.

Help your bathroom seem serene and clean with a crisp colour palette of blue and white.

The basic palette for this welcoming sitting room is a mix of calm grey-blue, white and navy. These sedate colours all work well together to create a relaxing space. Then, to bring the scheme to life, accessories in bright red are added; their glowing colour attracts attention and brings a feeling of warmth and cosiness to the scheme.

Quick trick

To add some liveliness to your scheme, choose cushions and ornaments in contrasting colours to the walls and furniture. They're easily replaceable when you want to update the scheme.

COLOUR AND LIGHT

The amount of light that your room receives from both natural and artificial sources plays an enormous part in how your chosen colours will look in the room at different times of the day – from bright daylight to when night falls.

Colours are dramatically altered by both natural and artificial light. The amount and type of light in the room will affect your colour choices, and also the mood of the completed room, so when considering different colours of paint, paper or fabrics make sure you know how they will look in the room both during the day and in the evening.

Before you choose your colour scheme it's important to take note of how much sunlight the room receives. Cool colours work well in sunny rooms with lots of natural daylight. If the room is hot in the summer, these cool shades keep the room looking fresh. Rooms that get little sunshine could be brightened up with a bright but pale shade of yellow, or warmed up with deep reds and oranges.

Daylight comes into a room from windows or glazed doors, meaning that unless the room has lots of windows the light source will be directional. Walls facing windows will appear lighter in colour than those adjacent to the windows. The window wall itself will be the darkest of all. The result is that your paint and paper will alter in colour from dark to light tones as the daylight moves around the room.

A room's lights are usually placed so that in the evening the walls will be more evenly lit. How you light a room can make an enormous difference both to how colours appear and to the mood the room evokes. This applies not only to the positioning of the lights, but also to the type. Just as a colour will look different in daylight and artificial light, the type of bulb will also affect colour perception. Halogen bulbs emit a white light that's similar to daylight, but standard household tungsten bulbs give out a warm, slightly yellow glow which warms up some colours, affecting the overall mood of the room. For more on this, see the lighting section, page 144 in Finishes and Furniture.

In this sitting room, pure white is mixed with accessories in off-white and ivory. The lack of colour throws the emphasis on texture and shape, and the smooth china and textured soft furnishings help create subtle pools of light and shadow throughout the space.

USING COLOUR TO DEFINE YOUR SPACE

Colour can help alter the apparent space of a room. For example, painting the walls of a small room a dark, warm shade will generally make the room feel smaller and cosier, while painting the same room with pure white will help the room feel light and airy.

Because warm shades of red, orange and yellow appear to advance, they can be used to make longer rooms appear shorter or wider: painting the furthest wall from the door in a warm shade gives the impression of a shorter, wider room.

As cool shades of blues and greens appear to recede, these colours can be used to help small rooms appear larger. Small attic rooms often benefit from having the walls and ceiling painted in the same light shade, so the angles of the sloping walls and ceilings are less obvious and the room appears more spacious.

All-white decorating schemes have a light and airy quality and help a room to appear larger than it is. To ensure an all-white room appears calm and tranquil rather than stark and harsh, choose a mix of white ingredients with a range of different textured surfaces. If you don't like white walls but want your rooms to appear spacious, go for pale blue. After white, it's the next best colour for increasing the sense of space.

ABOVE In this dining room, vibrant rust-orange paint on the walls appears to bring them closer, creating a feeling of warmth and cosiness.

RIGHT Cool pale blue walls are ideal for increasing the sense of space in this contemporary sitting room.

COMBINING COLOURS

Colours are not only influenced by light but by each other, and how successfully a colour scheme works in a room often depends on getting the balance and combination of shades and tones right.

CREATING HARMONY

The easiest way to create a calm and harmonious scheme is to decorate using several different tones of the same colour. Neutral colour schemes often rely on this device, varying the tones from dark to light so there's plenty of visual interest but little or no colour contrast. Another way to ensure a harmonious room scheme is to select three colours adjacent to each other on the colour wheel. Pick similar tones of each shade to create a scheme in a mix of colours that make natural neighbours.

Quick trick
Stuck for inspiration with your colour scheme? Take a look at your favourite pictures or paintings: they could provide you with the perfect colours for your rooms.

ADDING CONTRAST

If you think your harmonious scheme needs a little more excitement, try adding a contrasting colour into the mix. Contrasting colours, also known as complementary colours, sit opposite to each other on the colour wheel: blue opposite orange, red opposite green, and yellow opposite purple.

A small amount of contrasting colour will successfully liven up a scheme, but large areas of two contrasting colours may be jarring and hard to live with. The most successful schemes are those where one colour or tone predominates, leaving the other to take on a minor yet supporting role.

One of the best ways to ensure that a scheme of mixed colours works effectively is to choose different tones of the two contrasting shades. Pick light tones of one shade for the room's main background colour and contrast them with dark shades of the other for the decorative accents. For example, dark purple provides a good contrasting accent colour in a pale yellow room.

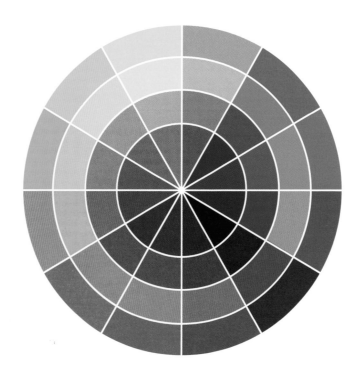

Pale tones of pink, cream and oatmeal sit easily together, and provide a relaxing backdrop for this calm sitting room. Splashes of chocolate brown bring a note of richness to the scheme while still staying within the same palette of colours.

Here, the glossy orange kitchen cabinets are the room's focal point and a small amount of blue, provided by the petrol blue upholstery on the chairs, provides a perfect contrast. The pale backdrop of the walls and floor, and the lightness of the room itself prevent the strong colours from becoming uncomfortably overwhelming.

BLACK AND WHITE

Classic black and white has to be the most dramatic colour combination we can decorate with. Used exclusively, these two extreme neutral shades can create a stylish and eye-catching decorative scheme.

Used together, black and white create arresting and dramatic room schemes which look smart, classic and grand.

Black and white colour schemes usually work best where white is the predominant shade, with black used to pick out details. In practice this means choosing white as the background colour for the walls and flooring, and often also for large pieces of furniture such as the sofa. Then steadily add a mix of black and white patterned items or black accessories into the scheme, such as cushions, vases and rugs, until you begin to see that a balance between the two shades has been reached. You can also restrict or increase the amount of black in the room by choosing fabric patterns which are either white-on-black (more black) or black-on-white (more white).

White is the predominant background colour in this sitting room; it's been used for the walls, floor, sofa and curtains. Adding a large-scale black and white patterned rug and white-on-black blinds injects pattern and drama, while a mix of printed black and white floral cushions and lots of monochrome accessories completes the look.

PERIOD PALETTES

Many historical paint colours are still popular today. If you're searching for a particular look for your home, do some detailed research into that style or era to ensure you choose colours that not only suit your home but also appeal to your decorating style. Period palettes usually concentrate on three historical periods:

Georgian (1714–1837): Subtle, understated colours from this era create an elegant look. Pale minty greens and muted blues or sedate shades of cream, stone and pink were used to create restrained, sophisticated rooms.

Victorian (1837–1901): Deep, rich colours are key to creating rooms with highly decorative, ornate appeal. Deep tones of red, green and blue were popular for formal rooms, and painted on to panelling or embossed wallpaper in corridors and hallways.

Edwardian and Art Deco (1901–39): During this period, bright and permanent paint colours became more available and affordable. From the deep, often military-inspired shades of bright red, forest green and dark grey of the early 1900s to the soft pastel shades favoured during the 1920s, this period includes many versatile colours for homes which can be reinterpreted for today's décor.

Heritage colours are versatile enough to suit both traditional and contemporary homes, such as these muted beiges inspired by the Georgian palette.

PATTERNS

From large-scale floral fabrics to subtle speckled work surfaces, patterns bring movement and pace to a room scheme, and even the smallest or slightest pattern makes a contribution to the overall look of a room.

We usually associate pattern with wallpapers and soft furnishings, but look around you and you will find a huge assortment of patterns in any room, from bathroom tiles and kitchen work surfaces to decorative details such as lampshades and curtain tie-backs.

The size and the repeat of the pattern will influence how you use it. Some patterns have an obvious repeat, such as wallpapers and fabrics with a distinct motif that can be seen repeating along the roll or across the width. Other patterns are less distinct, such as wallpapers with a swirly, interlocking pattern which, once hung, appears to flow seamlessly across the wall.

LARGE PATTERNS

Large-scale patterns dominate rooms, drawing the eye towards them. They look good used as a focal point in one area of a room, such as a two-tone damask wallpaper hung as an accent wall in a dining or living room, or a bold floral curtain fabric used to frame a

dramatic bay window. This single use of a pattern turns the pattern itself into a feature, drawing the eye towards it. This look can be very effective, but it needs to be surrounded by plenty of unadorned space.

If you're unsure where to start, use large-scale patterns with caution, especially if the room is on the small size.

Busy, multi-coloured patterns are wonderful as accents to a room scheme, but overwhelm a room if they are used on every surface. Keep the background colour plain, and ensure the patterns used are chosen in colours that coordinate with each other.

LEFT Choosing a large-scale patterned wallpaper adds drama and movement to a room, especially if the pattern is chosen in two contrasting shades. Simple furnishings let the paper shine.

ABOVE Patterns can be used to lead the eye onwards. Here the doorway is framed with a detailed wallpaper pattern, which highlights the doorway itself and draws attention to the dining area beyond.

KEY STYLE FEATURES – USING LARGE PATTERNS

Large-scale patterns are bold and eye-catching in living spaces.

The soft aqua of the remaining walls pick up the colour in the wallpaper, and the rug adds further colour, pattern and texture in a more subtle way.

This single accent wall allows the pattern to be a key part of the décor without it dominating the room scheme.

Accessories chosen in deep toning shades add interest to a room.

KEY STYLE FEATURES – USING SMALL PATTERNS

Mix delicate patterns with blocks of plain colour.

The bedstead and wood panelling provide their own linear patterns that help balance the feminine florals.

Plain white linen is a classic choice that works well with patterned fabrics.

Silky scatter cushions add a touch of sheen.

Floral curtains bring colour pattern to the room.

BELOW This pastel blue polka-dot wallpaper is a classic geometric design. It lends cheerfulness and country-style charm to this corner of a busy kitchen/dining room.

RIGHT Funky patterned cushions are the focal point in this room. The chair and wall provide the background colours, while the cushions and curtains mix and match in coordinating shades of bright pink, pale blue and lime green.

ADDING PATTERN

Layers of patterns will create a room scheme with depth. Fabric collections frequently have several patterns all related to the same theme, such as a large-scale floral, a sprigged floral, and a plain textured weave. Pick one to be the main pattern in the scheme, then add the others in smaller quantities for a coordinated yet highly patterned scheme. For an eclectic look, pick patterns with similar colours or themes, then mix several together.

Patterns used as detailing help define the space around them. Patterned trim on plain scatter cushions or a bedspread will add variety and emphasize their shape; patterned braid along the bottom of a simple roller blind or a patterned border of tiles in a plain-tiled bathroom draws the eye towards the object and helps create visual interest in the room.

SMALL PATTERNS

Small-scale wallpaper patterns, used on every wall, can help small bedrooms and bathrooms appear warm and cosy. Geometric patterns, whether simple stripes or funky retro graphics, look wonderful on wallpaper, where you can appreciate the mathematical symmetry of the design, as long as the walls are straight and true. A horizontal striped wallpaper will accentuate the height of a room, while a striped stair runner will draw attention towards and up the stairs.

Stripes and checks mix well with each other, and with other simple designs such as polka dots and stars. They are also good companions to florals and toile de Jouy patterns, provided that the colours of the various elements coordinate.

BRIGHT IDEAS
WAYS WITH COLOUR

It takes confidence to combine colours successfully. One of the best ways to work with colour is to start with a small selection of coordinating and contrasting colours, known as a palette. Here are six key palettes, each used to create three different looks in the same room. Each palette has only seven shades, but by mixing and matching the colour tones within each one it's possible to create rooms that are wildly different from each other in both colour and style.

SUMMER FRESH

This palette mixes vibrant summery shades of coral, lime green, pale blue and warm purple, which are kept cool, calm and collected with soothing cream, sandy and grey-toned neutrals, to create three easy-to-live with colour schemes.

CLASSIC GOOD LOOKS

For a sitting room that's calm, classic and up to date, use the neutral cream shades of the palette together, then add a lift of colour by including the pale blue shade throughout the room.

Sprigged floral wallpaper has timeless appeal, and the pale blue on cream brings colour and pattern to the walls without dominating the room.

Painting beneath the dado rail helps anchor the room's colour scheme.

A pretty mix of scatter cushions adds splashes of colour to the cream sofa upholstery fabric.

Choosing fabrics from the same collection as the wallpaper coordinates the look.

A pale cream carpet provides a neutral background, while the inexpensive striped rugs inject pattern and colour.

FRESH AND LIVELY

Here, the coral shade takes centre stage. Coral and blue accessories bring some real liveliness to the room, while the dark cream shade, which has sandy overtones, adds a sense of calm restraint. The completed room has a summery feel that will last throughout the year.

Neither too pink nor too orange, this coral shade brings a sense of summer warmth to the sitting room.

The bookcase has been painted to match the sofa, providing some neutral colour to balance the scheme.

Contrasting colours, such as these blue and coral scatter cushions, add an element of vibrancy to a room scheme.

Painting the floorboards with the palest cream shade adds a touch of seaside boardwalk charm to the room.

DARK AND DRAMATIC

For a sophisticated sitting room that's filled with drama, go for a mix of blue and purple, complemented by neutral notes of grey and cream.

The combination of pale cream curtains and a grey Roman blind is a simple and effective window treatment.

The large expanses of patterned wallpaper means it's important to keep the rest of the room virtually pattern-free, to avoid clashes and over-fussiness.

Pale blue cushions add a mimimal amount of bright colour to lift the scheme.

The remaining furniture is deliberately pared down in style: a basic metal standard lamp and modern side table add a contemporary touch.

SEASIDE ESCAPE

Imagine a clifftop walk overlooking a dramatic sea view, and be inspired to decorate your home with these seascape tones. The blues range from a deep stormy hue to a calming pale shade, while the natural tones are livened up with bright orange and bold green.

RETRO LOOKS

This sitting room picks three neutrals from the palette, grey, off-white and dark brown, and one vibrant colour, the bright rusty-orange, and mixes them to create an eye-catching room that has retro appeal.

Fresh, off-white walls are easy to live with and help lift the scheme.

The accessories have been chosen to bring lively colour to the room and coordinate with the overall scheme.

Choosing a patterned fabric in warm tones of orange and brown draws attention to the room's large windows.

Cool grey furniture looks sophisticated, while the cushions add a touch of warm colour.

Practical and contemporary, the walnut floor warms up the room scheme. The floor is made cosier underfoot by the shaggy orange rug.

BLUE AND BOLD

Choosing one bold pattern for your room is a great way to start. This blue and white fabric with its dramatic leaf motif pattern forms the basis for this scheme.

An accent wall of deep blue brings a dramatic injection of colour to the room. To avoid overpowering the room, the adjacent wall is painted pale grey.

Tiny touches of orange, which is the complement of blue on the colour wheel, add vibrancy.

White furnishings bring a light touch to the room, helping to lift the scheme and contrasting with the patterned fabric of the blinds and cushions.

NATURAL ELEGANCE

This neutral room scheme is in complete contrast to the previous room, and it's hard to believe that the colours come from the same palette. Here only the pale grey and off-white shades have been chosen, to create a natural-hued scheme that's filled with subtle pattern and texture.

The delicately patterned wallpaper on the fireplace wall is purposely similar to, but not the same as, the fabric used for the curtains and cushions.

A neutral scheme needs texture and pattern to be successful. Although the curtain fabric is neutral in colour it has a bold floral design. The upholstered footstools add some extra seating as well as bringing further pattern into the room.

A shaggy rug brings some textural interest and feels great underfoot.

ESSENCE OF SPRING

Spring flowers are the inspiration for this eye-catching palette. The colours of springtime floral favourites such as tulips, crocuses and hyacinths are visible in the vibrant pink and purple shades. Warm tones of woodland brown and pale cream balance the sugary brights.

style and colour

RELAX IN STYLE

This design uses the neutrals from the palette as the starting point for its scheme, with a dose of lime green to bring lively colour to this relaxing bedroom.

The geometric pattern adds a touch of retro charm to the room's overall look. Choosing the fabric in this zingy lime green colourway injects some vibrant colour into the mix.

Chocolate-brown furniture provides a calm backdrop: picking one statement piece such as this mirrored chest of drawers adds an unexpected twist.

Layering the bed with textured blankets and bedlinen in neutral shades makes the bed look inviting, and adds visual interest to the classic scheme.

AQUA DELIGHT

Aqua is a cheerful, springtime colour that works well with both neutral cream and chocolate brown, as well as brighter shades of pink. Here the four shades are mixed together to create a fresh and modern scheme.

One accent wall painted in the bright aqua shade is all that's needed to bring some modern colour to the room's walls. Light, bright and joyful, the colour lifts the whole scheme.

Dark wooden furniture has classic good looks and will stand the test of time. It also coordinates well with the neutral flooring.

Cushions and throws provide more colours from the bright end of the palette, without the need to decorate.

MODERN BRIGHTS

This colour-filled bedroom uses all the bright shades from the palette, mixing hot pink with lime green, aqua and purple. The exuberance is kept in check with a balancing background of cream, ensuring the overall look pulls together successfully.

The multi-coloured floral wallpaper behind the bedhead provides the focal point for the room's décor.

Choosing plain fabric for the curtains is essential, as these help prevent the scheme from being too busy. However, there's no need to be reticent in colour choice; this hot pink works perfectly with the colours in the rest of the room.

A mix of colourful bedlinen echoes the tones of the wallpaper, adding pattern.

AUTUMN HUES

This gentle palette is filled with colours reminiscent of a misty autumnal woodland walk. Four soft neutrals mix well with the stronger shades of aubergine, pale lime green and nut brown and provide a selection of colour combinations that are easy to work with.

CALM ELEGANCE

A pale lilac shade is the background wall colour in this modern sitting room, in which deep brown and aubergine provide extra colour depth.

The curtains bring some pattern to the room. Adding extra cushions on the sofa, made from the same fabric, helps provide a visual link between the two.

Glassware chosen in a warm shade of aubergine coordinates with the colours chosen for the room, and its rich colour gives a warm glow when it catches the light.

A nest of chocolate brown and metal tables coordinates with the central coffee table and provides plenty of extra surface space.

A contemporary rug adds both pattern and texture to the floor.

PURPLE HAZE

This dramatic colour scheme makes the most of the bright shades in the palette, combining the natural contrasts, lime and purple, with calming tones of nut brown and clotted cream.

The richly patterned lime-green curtains provide a touch of theatre and the colour contrasts perfectly with the aubergine walls.

Purple walls are not for the faint-hearted, but provided they are balanced with enough neutral shades, as here, they don't need to overwhelm the room.

Glass tables are light and reflective, providing surface space without adding extra colour to the scheme.

A contemporary rug in earthy shades of brown helps anchor the room's décor.

LIGHT AND AIRY

If aubergine and lime aren't your colours, then this palette still provides plenty of choice. This natural toned scheme combines the neutral shades of white, cream and fawn, offset by bursts of rich dark brown, so that the finished room feels filled with warmth and life.

The scatter cushions and throws have been mixed and matched to bring some contrasting texture to the room's scheme – a neutral scheme needs to be lifted with extra texture.

A sculptural table lamp looks great and provides visual interest.

A leather-covered tray and wicker log basket introduce further interesting textures.

This footstool is covered with a fabric that coordinates with the rest of the room's décor.

FIELDS OF COLOUR

Outdoors in the countryside in the height of summer, red, green and yellow mix harmoniously, and you can recreate the same carefree colour combinations at home. Green and red is a classic pairing; mix in a little pink and a deep yellow, then add a selection of muted neutrals.

MEADOW FRESH
Cool greens look wonderful with white. Fawn and beige anchor the scheme and provide base notes of neutral colour, while bursts of bright pink create a lively colour contrast in this fresh sitting room.

① Cool green walls bring freshness and an air of calm relaxation to the room.

The simple blind brings subtle pattern and colour to the window area.

These cheerful floral cushions provide the perfect balance to the more sombre checks used for the armchair and blind.

Checked upholstery brings smart geometric pattern to the room; this tweed check is reminiscent of cloth used by gentlemen tailors.

OPULENT CHARM

Mixing large patterns takes daring and flair. A large-scale wallpaper used on one wall provides lots of colour, pattern and interest, while the curtains and cushions each add their own colourful input.

A dramatic wallpaper, used on one accent wall only, adds a sense of opulence to the room.

Using a patterned fabric as a deep border on the curtains, rather than for the entire length, means the pattern does not overwhelm the window treatment.

The furniture is kept deliberately simple, allowing the other elements to be the focal point of the room.

The stone-coloured carpet provides a calm background to the riot of colour above.

EASY LIVING

Patterns and colours take a back seat as off-white and stone grey combine to create a contemporary sitting room that's filled with laid-back style.

Adjacent walls painted in two different shades of quiet neutrals add a sense of subtle movement to the scheme.

The sofa is the place to introduce splashes of brights to liven up the scheme.

A modern glass coffee table takes pride of place, and is perfect for displaying coloured-glass accessories.

Stone-coloured carpet, topped with a soft off-white rug, adds subtle texture and neutral tones to the scheme.

CHINA BRIGHTS

Pink-toned tea cups and brown earthenware jugs, blues from Wedgwood to willow pattern – the colours of traditional china lend themselves to this palette. The dominant shades are fuchsia pink and navy blue, supported by tones of pale blue, baby pink, chocolate and cream.

CLASSICAL ELEGANCE

An ornate toile wallpaper, chosen in a vibrant shade of fuchsia, is a highly decorative choice for these sitting-room walls. The scheme is balanced by keeping all other shapes and designs very simple.

The natural linen curtains are deliberately low-key. A simple ribbon trimming in bright fuchsia, stitched along the length of each curtain, is a clever decorative touch.

The mirror has a simple design, adding a sense of elegance and decorum to the room.

Leaving the floor free from rugs lets the neutral, wheat-coloured carpet offset the colourful wallpaper.

NAUTICAL AIRS

Plains and stripes in shades of blue are mixed together to create a sitting room with a distinctly nautical air. Dark chocolate brown and rich cream are the warming background shades.

Bold striped curtains look crisp and fresh. The eyelet tops add a nautical feel.

The decorative bottles are a perfect find for this room; their stripes and colours mimic the shades and patterns used throughout.

Scatter cushions, stitched from a mix of different striped fabrics, give the plain sofa a jaunty air.

A TOUCH OF THEATRE

Dark blue walls and luxurious heavy curtains combine to create a living room that's filled with drama. Fuchsia highlights add to the rich colour scheme, while a chocolate leather sofa is comfortable and inviting.

With its flowing design, the wallpaper pattern brings movement to the room, and prevents the dark walls from appearing oppressive.

Mirrored furniture and shiny accessories fill the room with sparkle and gleam, preventing the dark shades from appearing gloomy.

Silk cushions in jewel shades brighten the brown leather sofa.

A contemporary rug, chosen in a hot pink shade, livens up the floor space.

ASSESS YOUR SPACE

USING YOUR SPACE

When it's time to redecorate it's tempting to reach straight for the paint pot or head to the sales, but to get the scheme right and avoid expensive mistakes it's crucial to spend time planning your project before you start.

A bookshelf acts as a physical divide, screening this home-office area from the rest of the room. The extra storage space provided is handy for, and accessible from, both the living and working areas.

We require our homes to assume many roles, from home office to family home, from private sanctuary to party zone. Before you start redecorating, it's important to establish how you use a room on a day-to-day basis so that you can make the redesign successful on a practical as well as an aesthetic level. Thinking about the available space and how you use it will help to ensure that the finished room will not only look wonderful but also suit the way you live your life at home.

Then think about the reasons why you want to redesign the room. What is it about the current layout that you find frustrating or isn't working? If you love to cook but can't see to prepare food, think about the lighting in your kitchen. If there's never enough clear space in the hallway, do you need to do more than simply putting up coat hooks? Is the spare room more frequently used as an office than as a place for overnight guests to stay? If your children are older, can they share rooms or would they prefer a separate study-bedroom? By asking yourself questions such as these you will be able to find the solutions to the problems. The key is to be honest with yourself and choose a look that feels right for you.

YOUR MULTI-TASKING HOME

Rooms often serve several purposes, so look at how you actually use each room, rather than making assumptions based on what it's called. Do you do most of your living in the living room ... or in the kitchen?

What time of day is the room used?

Not all rooms are used equally throughout the day. If you're at home during the day working or caring for children you may never set foot in the bedroom or dining area. For families the kitchen, bedrooms and living rooms become filled with activity after school, and for most of us the sofa in the living room and the tub in the bathroom are our sanctuaries to help us wind down in the evening. The time of day that you use the room will influence not only your colour choices for the walls and fabrics, but also the designs and styles of furniture which you need. (See pages 40–41, for tips on how light can alter the colours in a room.)

KITCHENS

A kitchen/dining room is a place for cooking, entertaining, laundry, paperwork, homework and playing. It's a hardworking space that also needs to be welcoming.

Those who love cooking for friends appreciate the ease a kitchen/dining room creates for the host. Guests can mix freely in the dining area, or help with cooking, and the meal is prepared in a sociable, informal manner, which suits today's lifestyles. Nowadays family kitchens are often the hub of the home, where everyone congregates to socialize, play, do personal admin or homework and, of course, cook. Even the smallest kitchen can benefit from the tiniest of dining spaces: it can be as a basic as a stool and a flip-down table fixed to the wall.

If your budget stretches to structural work, you may want to consider increasing the physical space so there's room for everyone and all their activities. If not, careful planning of the area can result in a room that suits every member of the family.

Kitchen islands are useful devices because they can not only store kitchenalia, dinnerware and occasionally appliances such as a sink or a hob, but also provide a physical divide between the hard-working kitchen part of the room and the dining area. Open shelves are perfect for giving kitchens a relaxed, custom-built look, and they cost far less than wall-mounted kitchen units. Fill the shelves with attractive crockery and glassware, and you will give your kitchen an unfitted look that's right up to date.

You will need space for: a table; chairs; cooking and food preparation; appliances; storing food, kitchenware and dinnerware.

You might want space for: toy storage; a TV or music system; a pet basket; a home office; wall space for calendars, noticeboard, clock.

THIS SMALL KITCHEN makes best use of the available space, ensuring there's room for both cooking and dining.

A long wall shelf keeps the worktops clutter-free.

A utensil rail makes good use of the wall space and keeps the utensils close to hand.

Clear work surfaces mean there's plenty of space for preparing food.

Deep baskets are a good choice for storing pans and their lids.

LIVING ROOMS

Living rooms are for relaxing and socializing, but also for eating, drinking, watching TV and listening to music, entertaining, ironing and playing.

Whether the room is large or small, a well-planned living room makes the most of the space so that it is a relaxing and welcoming room. If you're out all day at work, it's important that you've got a room where you can open the door, collapse on the sofa, put on the TV or some music, and do nothing. If you love entertaining, make sure there's enough seating to comfortably fit extra guests, even if it's as simple as pulling out a few large, squashy floor cushions.

A sofa (or two) is considered an essential part of a living room, so plan for a new one carefully. As well as the design of the sofa's shape, the comfort factor and the style and colour of the upholstery, the size of the sofa is incredibly important – too big and it will dwarf the room, too small and it will look out of place and won't seat as many people as you had hoped.

Organize storage so that toys, DVDs, books and magazines are easily found yet out of the way when they're not needed. Custom-built cabinetry designed for your needs is the ideal, but ready-made shelving units, either open or in cupboards to conceal their contents, work just as well and help prevent clutter from taking over the room. A large coffee table with storage space beneath is another useful item. Keep some space free to display pictures, photographs and ornaments, which add a personal touch to the room.

> **You will need space for:** a sofa or comfy chairs; a coffee table; a TV and/or music system; some freestanding lighting.
>
> **You might want space for:** toys and books; side tables; lamps; a fireplace; wall space for pictures, mirrors, ornaments; musical instruments; DVD and CD storage; speakers.

THIS SITTING ROOM provides plenty of seating for family and guests, and also includes a home office and fireplace.

A contemporary flueless fire means the room has the warmth of a real fire despite the absence of a working chimney.

A fold-down desk provides a compact home-office area

There's enough space for a generously proportioned sofa, plus two armchairs.

BEDROOMS

Bedrooms are not only for sleeping but for dressing, reading, playing and getting some privacy from the rest of the house.

For parents, the bedroom can be the only room where privacy is guaranteed. If your home is busy and hectic, try to keep your bedroom as calm and as furniture-free as possible. Even if you don't subscribe to the minimalist aesthetic, remember that the only essential item you need in your bedroom is a bed. However, it's likely you will also need clothes-storage space, so plan this carefully to ensure that there's space to put everything away, helping keep any surfaces, chairs and even the floor free from unnecessary clutter.

Your bed should take priority; always choose the largest possible bed that will suit the available space, and the most comfortable mattress you can afford. If space is tight, think laterally; use the space beneath a bedstead for storing out-of-season clothes, or store these elsewhere, for example in a guest-bedroom wardrobe. Avoid piling books high on bedside tables by adding small bookshelves, and create a personal note in the room by displaying family photos and mementoes on walls or shelving. Keeping floor space clear of furniture will help the room feel more spacious than it is.

> **You will need space for:** a bed; and probably clothes-storage space.
> **You might want space for:** bookshelves; underbed storage; bedside tables and reading lights; wall space for pictures; surface space for ornaments and photographs; a dressing table.

THIS CALM BEDROOM has been kept relatively furniture- and clutter-free, which helps to create a relaxing atmosphere and aid a good night's sleep.

Sheer curtains help keep the room sunny and bright.

The tall storage unit provides just enough clothes-storage space, while the top is perfect for toiletries.

The low bedside table has surface space for a pretty table lamp and bedtime book.

A cotton valance hides underbed drawers from view; these provide valuable yet discreet extra storage space.

Plenty of floor space helps the room appear spacious.

CHILDREN'S ROOMS

For children, their bedrooms are their havens. Their needs also change over the years, so take a flexible approach and be prepared to alter the room's layout as your children grow up.

Babies and extremely young children don't need huge rooms, but if you haven't space for a separate playroom it can be worthwhile devoting a larger than necessary room for pre-school children so there is also room to store all their toys. Sharing may suit younger members of the family, and putting two children in together could free up a bedroom to be used as a guest bedroom or home office.

Because young children spend so much time playing on the floor it's important to keep the room relatively furniture-free. They'll need accessible storage and a comfortable bed; bunk beds can be ideal as they sleep two while taking up little floor space. Buying child-sized pieces of furniture can be a false economy, so if in doubt buy standard-size wardrobes and chests of drawers, as it won't be long before the child will be needing the storage space.

For teenagers, bedrooms are their own space where they can escape from the rest of the family. As well as a bed and a desk they'll need space for a computer, music system and whatever hobbies they enjoy. Letting them choose the décor gives them an opportunity to work out what aspects of design appeal to them, and allows them to put their personal stamp on their individual space.

Young children need space for: a bed; clothes storage; child-accessible toy storage; floor space to play.
Older children need space for: a bed; clothes storage; wall space for pictures and school notices; a desk and chair.

assess your space

LIGHT, BRIGHT AND AIRY, this roomy nursery will be easy to adapt as the baby grows older.

A generously sized wardrobe means there's room for larger sizes of clothes.

The room has space for a full size bed when the time comes to remove the cot.

A rug on the wooden floor means time spent playing will be comfy for small knees.

The space under the cot is used for extra storage.

BATHROOMS

Nowadays bathrooms are viewed as our sanctuaries rather than simply functional rooms. Large bathtubs provide a place to wind down, while powerful showers are instantly invigorating.

Bathrooms are often the smallest rooms in the house, but whatever the size of your bathroom the layout will need careful planning. Sanitaryware such as bathtubs, shower enclosures and basins come in a huge variety of shapes and sizes, and once they're in place it's difficult and costly to move them. The existing layout of the drainage and plumbing may dictate the arrangement of the new bathroom as it may prove too expensive to reroute the piping.

Even if you cannot change the layout of the room, you can completely alter the look of a new bathroom by opting for luxurious sanitaryware and glamorous fittings. If space allows, go for a bath and a shower, but ensure that there's still plenty of space to move around the room in comfort. One space-saving solution can be to go for a separate WC away from the main bathroom; this can also be helpful in busy homes where the bathroom gets heavy traffic and is in constant use in the evenings and mornings. Consider also your storage needs; a place for towels and toiletries is a must, and a cabinet beneath the basin uses this space well.

WITH SPACE at a premium, it's important to organize the bathroom so that it includes all the necessary elements and is also a relaxing place in which to spend time.

In small bathrooms, an all-white colour scheme keeps the room feeling as light and spacious as possible.

Placing a shower attachment above a bath ensures there is room for both a tub and a shower.

A heated towel rail is useful for warming the room and drying towels.

Vinyl flooring is a practical floor choice that's watertight and easy to clean.

Wooden surfaces add a luxurious element and the rich colour brings warmth to the room's overall look.

EXTRA ROOMS

If you're lucky to have a spare room in the house, be flexible about its use. The ideal homes are those which can adapt and change as the occupants' lives alter, whether it is the arrival of a new baby or the chance to set up a business from home.

Separate dining rooms tend to be used only during weekend evenings or on special occasions. With the right furniture, the dining room can also become a home office, a playroom, a homework room or even a guest bedroom.

Don't leave guest bedrooms empty; they can accommodate wardrobes to hold extra clothes and shelves for extra books, files and magazines you want to keep, or be used to create a dedicated home office space that's separate from the rest of the house. If space is tight, sheds and garages can be adapted to become laundry rooms or home offices, freeing up much-needed space within the home.

In rooms that are going to be in use in more than one way at a time, think about how the furniture can be arranged to separate the room's functions. A strategically placed shelf unit can divide an office area from the relaxing part of the living room. Likewise, either mobile or permanent kitchen islands can help bridge the gap between the cooking and eating areas of a kitchen/dining room. Screens are invaluable to hide filing from view in home-office spaces or guest rooms.

A bookshelf acts as a physical divide, screening this home-office area from the rest of the room. The extra storage space the shelves provide is accessible from both the living and working areas.

Making extra space for children in so-called adult areas can be as simple as fixing a drop-leaf table to a convenient wall in a dining or sitting room. It provides a place to draw and paint near to the parents, and the table and chair can be easily folded away when they're not needed.

SHARING SPACE

Family homes need to be flexible. Be prepared to alter the rooms' functions as children get older, and try to take into account everyone's needs for both some shared space and some private space.

SHARING SPACE WITH CHILDREN

Young children like to be close to adults while they play, and so a defined play area either in the kitchen or living area can work well. Consider giving children – especially if you have two who can share a room – one of the larger bedrooms so they can play happily with friends and have plenty of room to store toys.

Older children need a place to do homework: this is often the kitchen or dining table. They also need space to play, relax and socialize within the main rooms of the house, and somewhere to store their belongings; this can range from a cupboard for sports equipment to wall space for displaying artwork.

SHARING SPACE WITH A PARTNER

A shared bedroom and bathroom means compromising on personal space and choice of décor. If one of you works from home, come to an arrangement on where the office equipment will live, and how it gets stored when not in use. Entertaining space for guests may be key, and so, even if there are only two of you eating together most nights, you may want to include a larger dining or entertaining area in your plans so you have room for guests when they are visiting. Agree on what will be stored and where, but be flexible and accept that your needs may differ.

MEASURING UP AND MAKING PLANS

Planning how a room will be laid out so that everyone will be able to use it comfortably is an essential part of interior design. Key to getting this right is knowing, rather than guessing, how much space you have and what will fit in.

DRAWING A PLAN

Drawing accurately measured scale plans of your rooms mean you can experiment with different furniture arrangements to find the most practical and most appealing combination. It's vital you get the measurements and drawing correct to avoid any mistakes when shopping, so follow these pointers for easy plan drawing.

TO START

Pick a measurement system: choose either imperial or metric measurements, and stick to this system throughout to avoid making mistakes.

Choose a scale: for living rooms and bedrooms, a scale of 1:50 is usually most workable: this means in practice that 2 cm on your plan will represent 1 m of your room's dimensions. If you're working in imperial it will be easier to adjust this scale slightly to 1:48, so that 1 in on your plan is equal to 4 ft of the full size.

CHECKLIST
You will need:
- A4 squared graph paper
- retractable tape measure
- pencil
- ruler
- eraser

MEASURING UP

First, draw a rough sketch of the room on a piece of paper. Measure the length and width of the room and note these measurements on the rough sketch. Then walk around the room with a tape measure, measuring accurately and noting down the location and dimensions of all the features, including:

- windows and doors, including the width of those that open into the room
- projection and location of any fireplaces, chimney breasts and stub walls.
- existing power and phone points, and light switches
- in kitchens and bathrooms, the location of plumbing and drainage
- any extra specific details that need to be taken into account, such as built-in furniture or changes in floor level between different parts of the room.

Transfer the measurements on to graph paper, using a pencil and ruler, ensuring you include all the details.

HOW THE PLAN CAN HELP YOU

Trying out layouts Make templates of furniture by drawing to scale their basic shapes on to graph paper, then cutting them out. Play around with arrangements until you find one that works. You will be able to evaluate what's the best furniture arrangement, and what will successfully fit into the room, without either moving heavy furniture or making an expensive mistake.

Marking the 'flow' of the room This shows how you and guests walk around the room, and can help you visualize where to place furniture. For example, a room with two sets of doors should have a clear pathway between the doors, while in a dining room there should be enough space for everyone to push back their chairs as they leave the table.

Marking the 'sweep' of doors You will need to take into account the space the doors take up as they open and close to avoid placing furniture in their way.

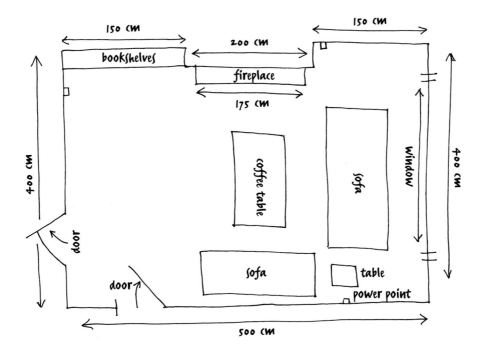

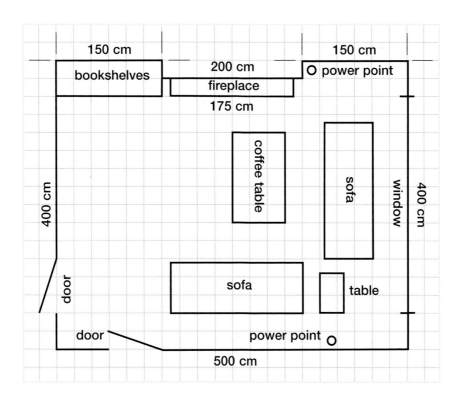

UNDERSTANDING HOW YOUR ROOM WILL WORK

Writing lists of how you want to use the room and drawing scale plans are invaluable practical first steps, but creating a room that's pleasant to live in also means taking into account how it works on a daily basis.

Your room isn't static. It has movable parts, including chairs, windows and doors (internal, wardrobe, cupboard and cabinet) as well as drawers and window treatments such as curtains and blinds, which will need to be accessed both during the daytime and in the evening. You need to be able to reach these easily, and to allow for any space they take up when they are open or closed. Remember, too, that the room is a living space, filled with people who'll add their physical presence and their belongings. While in the room, they'll use and move furniture, altering the room as they do so.

The furniture you choose should be appropriate for both the size of the room and its intended use as well as being a design that pleases you aesthetically – see Your Design Scheme for more information on how to choose the right furniture for your rooms.

GROUPING FURNITURE AND LEAVING SPACE
The basic rules for arranging furniture are down-to-earth and easy to remember:
☐ pick a focal point
☐ group furniture around it
☐ leave some space free.

Leaving space allows the room's design and layout to 'breathe' and, more practically, it enables you and your family and guests to move around the room freely.

It's also important to think about how the room looks as you enter it. Viewing the backs of furniture from the door can make a room appear unwelcoming. If one room leads directly into another, help the rooms flow easily by allowing a broad enough route through one room and into the next. A walkway approximately 1 m (3 ft) wide will allow easy access.

Placing the armchair at an angle to the sofa creates a convivial and informal seating arrangement. A circular coffee table helps the space flow.

SITTING ROOMS

Place sitting-room furniture in a group to encourage relaxed conversation, with enough surfaces within reach for lamps, glasses and books. Your main aim here is to create a welcoming space that's perfect for both relaxing and for entertaining.

Do: Leave enough space for guests to sit down easily • Make the furniture accessible from the door • Place coffee or side tables no more than 45 cm (18 in) away from the sofa and chairs to ensure they are within reach when you're seated. **Don't:** Place all the furniture against the walls; your room will look institutional, and the space between the furniture will inhibit relaxed conversation.

THIS COSY SITTING ROOM has a relaxed and welcoming layout.

The sofa faces the room's entrance, and the coffee table is within easy reach when seated.

There are plenty of surfaces for glasses and cups.

The armchair opposite is just close enough for easy conversation with guests.

COOKING AND EATING AREAS

In kitchens and dining rooms you need to incorporate easily accessible storage for dining essentials such as glassware, crockery and table linen. It's vitally important that the table and chairs leave enough room for your guests to sit comfortably at the table.

Do: Allow enough space – about 70–100 cm (28–40 in) – for chairs to be pushed back from the table • Appliances need access space; you will probably need to allow 65 cm (26 in) to open the oven door.

Don't: Place too many chairs around the table, or guests will feel cramped • Position furniture so it blocks access to cupboard doors.

THIS LARGE open-plan kitchen and living room has been carefully divided into distinct areas. Despite the room's many functions, there is plenty of space around the dining table for guests to dine in comfort.

Low pendant lighting above the dining table ensures there is plenty of ambient light to dine by.

White-painted walls in the kitchen area and red-painted walls in the dining area make a visual contrast that helps demarcate the two parts of the room.

A separate console table, placed by the wall at the head of the dining table, provides an extra surface for serving food and drinks.

BEDROOMS

In bedrooms the bed needs to be the right size for the room, which means you and your partner need to be able to get in and out of the bed with ease. Ensure that you have enough space to open chests of drawers and wardrobes.

Do: Allow about 80–100 cm (30–40 in) clearance around wardrobe doors and drawers • Fit sliding doors on fitted wardrobes to save floor space.
Don't: Cram too much furniture into a small bedroom; people need space in which to move around and get dressed, and double beds need to be accessible on both sides.

IN THIS BEDROOM, the contemporary metal four-poster bed makes a dramatic focal point. Despite the bed's large size, there is plenty of room on both sides to get in and out of it.

The bed frame is left free from drapes so the simple beauty of its structure can be appreciated.

Choosing reflective furniture helps bounce light around the room, and so makes the room appear larger.

Two small mirrored chests of drawers on either side of the bed double up as clothes storage and bedside tables, so reducing the need for a larger chest of drawers.

To avoid the feeling that the room is crammed with furniture, the other pieces are small and understated.

HOME OFFICES

Home offices need plenty of accessible storage, as well as a desk and a chair. If space is tight, use all the available wall space for storage racks and shelves. Allow at least 70 cm (28 in) of floor space for the chair when sitting at the desk.

Do: Ensure there are plenty of phone and power points close to the desk • In shared spaces, consider a room divider; it can be as simple as a folding screen.

Don't: Let office equipment dominate in a shared space with a dining room or bedroom.

A HOME OFFICE can be tucked into the smallest of spaces, provided you've measured the area and are sure you can fit in all you need. This corner provides an ideal spot for a pack-away office for short-term or occasional desk work.

Good light for working is essential; this angled light boosts light levels after dark or on a cloudy day.

Paperwork can be stored out of the way on the shelves and wire rack.

Simple foldaway furniture is easy to assemble when required, although it isn't suitable for long periods of office work.

BATHROOMS

Bathrooms need particularly careful measuring and planning before the main components are ordered and work begins, because fitted sanitaryware is a permanent fixture that can be expensive to alter once it has been installed. Existing pipework may also dictate the new design and layout.

Do: Remember to allow sufficient clearance around the sanitaryware (see box, right).

Don't: Cram large-scale pieces into a small bathroom if you can't use them in comfort.

Typical dimensions and clearances

Bathtubs: average 152–170 cm long and 70–76 cm wide (60–66 in x 28–30 in). Depending on the room layout, you will need to allow around 70 cm (28 in) clearance along the side.

Shower trays: typically 90 x 90 cm (35 x 35 in); allow 70 cm (28 in) clearance in front of the cubicle.

WCs: about 70 cm (28 in) front to back, and they need 60 cm (24 in) clearance space in front of them.

Basins: come in a wide range of sizes. and so there is one suited to most spaces. Whichever you pick, you will need to allow at least 70 cm (28 in) in front for comfort when using the basin.

WITH A WELL-THOUGHT-OUT room plan that includes built-in storage as well as a streamlined shower enclosure you will be able to create a relaxing shower room that's a pleasure to use.

A rounded corner unit makes good use of limited space and has no protruding corners.

Towels and toiletries don't need to be hidden away, and open shelving means there is no need to allow for door-opening space.

This laundry basket doesn't take up too much valuable space, and having it to hand will encourage the family not to leave discarded clothes strewn over the floor.

ATTIC AND LOFT ROOMS

Using the roof space can usefully increase your living area, but to realize this potential you need to think and plan carefully. Attic rooms in older homes are often cramped, low-ceilinged and with rarely more than one narrow window. Modern loft conversions may have more space but still need careful thought.

In both attic and loft rooms, optimum use of the space is key. A desk can fit into a low part of the room, but can you sit easily at the chair to work? A bed might fit under a dormer window, but can you easily get out of the bed and stand up straight? Always check you will be able to get new furniture up the stairs and into the room before you order it.

Furniture should be arranged around the highest part of the room, so that adults can move around the centre of the room in comfort. If this isn't possible, consider turning the room into a den for watching television, a children's playroom, or a storage room for out-of-season clothes.

The narrow sloping space under the eaves in attic rooms is often best turned into storage space. The shelves in this en suite loft bathroom turn the unused space into a handy place for storing toiletries and towels close to the basin.

A sloping roof can provide the perfect spot for an under-eaves bathroom, but ensure that the shower attachment is located with enough space for it to be used in comfort.

Get the look for less

While custom-built shelving can be designed to fit awkward spaces exactly, with some careful measuring you can find off-the-peg storage units that will slot into place. Cube storage is ideal for low spaces, or try a selection of baskets or small metal shelving units.

If the attic or loft room is small, treat the walls and ceilings as one, and use the same wallpaper or paint colour on both. This helps disguise any awkward angles. A favourite country-cottage look is to pick a toile de Jouy paper and use it on both walls and ceilings. Painting a dark room in a pale shade will help it appear lighter and more airy. Keep window treatments simple; blinds allow maximum daylight to enter the room, as do curtains on brackets that swing closed over the window rather than draw to one side.

assess your space

Placing the bed in the centre of this attic bedroom is a practical move as it takes advantage of the maximum headroom available, and ensures it's accessible from both sides. Hanging a highly patterned wallpaper on the far wall draws attention to the sloping ceiling, making a feature of the room's quirky architecture.

Alcoves

Alcoves make excellent storage space. Frequently found on either side of fireplaces, they are wonderful for bookshelves and also work well as display areas for treasured ornaments, or for collections of photographs or pictures. Custom-built shelves should be made to fit the space exactly, and be strong enough to hold whatever you're planning to store on them. (For more ideas on display, see Fast Fixes and Finishing Touches.)

Two simple chunky shelves fit this alcove perfectly, and are ideal for displaying a collection of pretty ornaments.

ROOM SIZES

Both large and small rooms need careful planning to make the most of their space, whether this involves fitting ingenious storage into a tiny kitchen or accommodating several different aspects of family life into a large living room.

If either the length or width of a room is less than 3 m (10 ft), this room is considered to be small. If either the length or width is greater than about 10 m (30 ft), this is considered a large room. A large room may work better divided into two distinct areas so the space is not wasted. Consider dual-purpose rooms, such as a living room with a reading area, a dining area or a TV area; a large kitchen can become a kitchen/dining room, or a home office can be incorporated into a large sitting room or dining room.

In a small room, floor space is likely to be tight, so don't forget to look upwards and use the upper wall space for storage. The dead space above a door can make an ideal location for a small bookshelf, while traditional clothes airers, suspended from the ceiling, are great for tiny utility rooms.

Whether your rooms are small or large, making scale plans can help you work out the best arrangement of the furniture without having to physically move it yourself, and help you see if new furniture will fit.

THIS LONG ROOM has been successfully split into two separate areas, one for relaxing and the other for dining. The separate areas, while distinct, flow together well; there's no barrier between the seating and eating parts of the room.

Armchair-style seats help the dining area feel an intrinsic part of the living room.

A circular dining table has a friendly, informal air.

Choosing the same fabrics for the sofa and dining chair cushions provides some coordination and helps the two parts of the room feel like one.

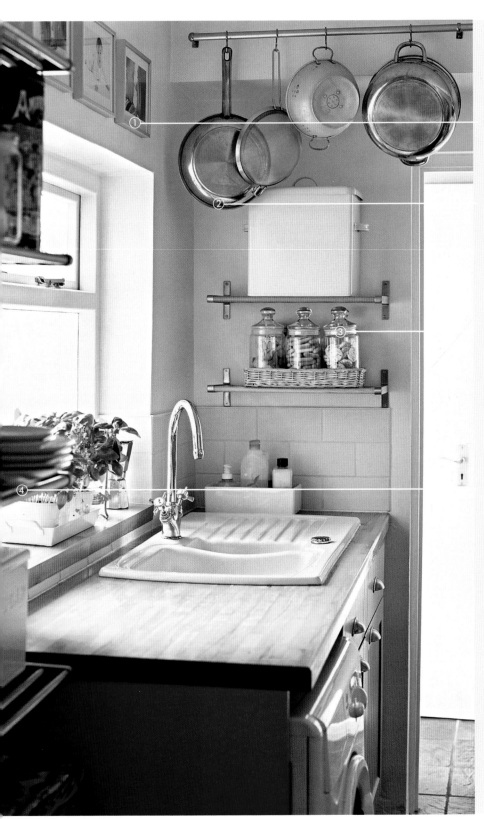

THIS NARROW galley kitchen makes the most of the available wall space.

There's no space wasted. The wall above the window is home to a series of framed family photographs.

A utensil rail, fixed high up, is the ideal place for storing bulky pans.

Narrow shelves fit the space on the far wall perfectly, and store dry foods safely away from the wet sink area.

Streamlined metal shelves are fitted into the corner of the room by the kitchen door, for storing crockery, glassware and foodstuffs.

ARCHITECTURAL FEATURES IN YOUR HOME

Architectural features in a home range from large elements, such as staircases and fire surrounds, to small details from ceiling roses to door mouldings. Features such as beams, ancient fireplaces and sloping ceilings can be both a blessing and a problem in older properties, while installing features can add interest to box-shaped modern rooms.

FIREPLACES

A fireplace is one of the best architectural features a room can have. An obvious focal point, the fire itself provides warmth and inviting light, while the surround and chimney breast can both be used to display ornaments and pictures that draw the eye to this part of the room.

REVITALIZING AN OLD FIREPLACE

Despite their appeal as a feature, fireplaces can seem drab and dreary if they are never used. Remedy this by changing the fire itself. If you never light the fire because you can't face the mess of coal or wood, opt instead for a modern gas or electric fire. Likewise, replace out-dated electric fires with either a modern flueless fire or a multi-fuel stove; you will find designs to fit every interior, from traditional to ultra-contemporary.

If you don't like the style of the surround, there are plenty of companies who offer restored original or reproduction alternatives, made from wood, stone or iron. You could also replace the fireplace entirely, opting for a completely new grate, hearth and surround. While the standard advice is to choose a replacement fireplace that suits the age and style of the room, a top-of-the-range contemporary fireplace can look stunning in a period setting, providing the room's furnishings and décor are also modern in style.

Resurrecting or replacing an old fireplace isn't always a possibility, but the chimney breast and hearth can still become the focal point of a room, even if there's no working fire in place. Use the space as a display area, placing vases, decorative balls or even a string of fairy lights in the hearth, and hang mirrors or paintings on the chimney breast above.

Quick trick
Cleaning and polishing a wood or iron surround can make all the difference to the finished look of a tired fireplace, while a coat of paint on an unloved pine surround can make the fireplace look up to date with little effort or expense.

INSTALLING A NEW FIREPLACE

This is one of the best ways to introduce character to a sitting room. The natural position for a living room fireplace is in the centre of the main wall. For the fireplace to become the heart of the room, ensure there's enough space to group comfy chairs, a sofa and a coffee table around it.

There are thousands of reproduction designs available, plus a wide choice of contemporary 'hole-in-the-wall' designs if you're looking for something a little more modern. Flueless fires mean it's possible to have a working fire on almost any internal wall.

AN OPEN HEARTH with a simple grate and an off-white wooden fire surround is all that's needed to turn this fireplace into the room's focal point.

The large square mirror with its deep natural wood frame suits the proportions and style of the fireplace.

Grouping the furniture around the fire adds to the room's cosy, intimate atmosphere.

IN THIS CONTEMPORARY sitting room, colour and ornaments turn an empty hearth into a decorative display area.

The chimney breast is home to a treasured piece of artwork.

The disused fireplace recess has been painted a cool blue to match the walls, and filled with logs so it looks the part.

A collection of elegant, contemporary vases on the hearth frames the fire recess.

STAIRCASES

Every two-storey home will have a staircase, but although they're an essential part of our homes they're often overlooked when planning a scheme for a hall or landing. The space around them is also often under-used, yet is ideal for display and storage.

Replacing a staircase is a big job and there are many safety regulations to observe, from the size of the treads to the distance between each banister; so unless you're desperate for a new staircase it's advisable to make the most of what is currently in place. Staircases need handrails for safety, and some floorings are not suitable due to the risk of slipping.

Insider info

Unless you have a very grand marble staircase, the banisters are likely to be the most notable feature. In older houses these have sometimes been covered over – check in case you have an attractive newel post and spindles concealed beneath bland boarding.

THIS COMPACT KITCHEN is fitted in place of an under-stairs cupboard, making a virtue of a space that was never used effectively. Custom-made units ensure best possible use of the tiny space.

Clever design makes a feature out of the sloping underside of the stairs.

Continuing the paint colour without a break helps incorporate the understairs area into the rest of the room, visually opening it up.

NEUTRAL COLOURS and a gleaming handrail on the staircase make this hallway light, bright and welcoming.

A collection of family portraits, in wooden frames, leads the eye up the stairs.

The banisters have been sanded and polished, and the turned newel post is a feature in its own right.

BRIGHTEN UP YOUR STAIRCASE

Polish wooden handrails so they gleam. If the wood is poor quality, or to give the staircase some rustic charm, paint or stain it a light colour which coordinates with the surrounding landing and hallway.

Jazz up a bland, dull stairwell with dramatic lighting. Lighting it cleverly from above will not only make the staircase safer to use, but will also provide a welcoming glow when you enter the house. Open-tread staircases can also be lit effectively and dramatically from below. The stairwell is the perfect place to display pictures, so use it as a family gallery, to display photos or pictures that everyone can see as they climb the stairs.

If the staircase descends directly into a room rather than a hallway, prevent it from dominating the room by painting it an unobtrusive colour. Help it become an integral part of the room by turning the space beneath into an open-plan living or storage area.

On the other hand, you might like to use the staircase as an architectural feature and emphasize its angular structure. Instead of fitted carpet or bare wood (which is very noisy), you could opt for a central runner. These come in a variety of styles, including colourful stripes and natural matting. Paint the edges of the treads and risers, either to match the surrounding woodwork or in a contrasting colour.

ARCHITECTURAL MOULDINGS

Architectural mouldings have a part to play in the overall appeal of a room, especially in an older property. Cornices and covings at the top of the walls and skirtings at the bottom hide the join between the walls, ceiling and floor and so provide a seamless visual flow between the room's surfaces.

Painting the ceiling white in this cottage bedroom has ensured that the beams stand out. Soft lilac walls and crisp white curtains make the room look fresh, while maintaining a traditional air in keeping with the age of the house.

COVING, ARCHITRAVE AND OTHER ARCHITECTURAL TRIMS

Older homes can have an unfinished look if the mouldings have been removed from walls and doors, so part of the restoration work may include replacing any missing mouldings. It is worthwhile researching appropriate styles.

In modern homes it is best to be cautious, as filling a room with added architectural details can add a sense of unnecessary fussiness. However, coving can be used to add interest to a plain, box-like room, while narrow skirting boards can be made deeper by fixing a length of profiled moulding above the existing board, and then repainting the entire skirting the same colour.

Pale blue tongue-and-groove panelling adds a touch of architectural interest to this entrance hall, lending the room a laid-back, country-style charm.

This same principle applies to simple door and window architraves, which can be made bigger using extra lengths of decorative moulding fitted around the existing architraves. This has the advantage of drawing attention to the window or door, while adding visual interest to a featureless room.

In today's homes, dado and picture rails usually have only decorative appeal, but they can be useful to break up large expanses of wall in long rooms.

BEAMS

In barns or older homes with beams, let the beams stand out. For a pared-down look, keep walls a pale neutral shade and, if the walls as well as ceiling are beamed, keep pictures on the wall to a minimum.

Beams that have been painted black can be professionally sandblasted to return them to their natural shade.

PANELLING

If the idea of wooden panelling makes you think of ancient homes from history books, then think again. Simple wooden tongue-and-groove cladding, made from an inexpensive softwood such as pine, is usually available from DIY stores or is relatively easy for a carpenter to make. It can be used either to dado height, picture rail height or from floor to ceiling to great effect in kitchens, hallways and bathrooms. It's ideal for covering less than perfect walls, helps hide pipes and insulation, and can be painted any shade you fancy.

BRIGHT IDEAS
ONE ROOM, THREE WAYS

If you feel your rooms could work harder for you, or if you're looking to change the present function of a room, then take a look at these clever room solutions. In each one, the space is the same but the furniture layout and décor have been given three different treatments.

ONE SITTING ROOM, THREE WAYS

Short of space? Get your sitting room to double up as a family room, a dining room or a home office and you will find that the room becomes a hive of activity.

assess your space

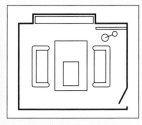

happy families

Plenty of practical storage means this room suits a family lifestyle, but can quickly be transformed for adults to enjoy in peace. The low storage unit beneath the window and the coffee table both provide homes for toys and games. Sliding panels pull across the window area, hiding any mess from view.

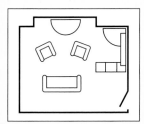

office corner

The working corner of this sitting room functions fully as a home office and yet does not dominate or distract from the seating area. The furniture suits a room that's used for both working and relaxing; the small armchair doubles as an office chair, while the bookshelves provide storage and define the two areas of the room.

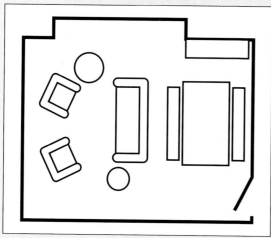

entertain in style

A dramatic accent wall highlights the dining area, while the seating area is situated to benefit from the sunlight. The tall storage unit provides a mix of shelves for display, and a cupboard for storing dining essentials, while the back of the roomy white sofa acts as a room divider, forming a physical barrier.

ONE DINING AREA, THREE WAYS

Large kitchen/dining rooms are versatile spaces that lend themselves to being organized as a family dining room, a room for entertaining or even a space for working from home.

assess your space

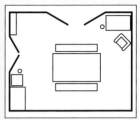

work from home

Furniture in the same style and similar wood for both the office and dining areas gives the room a unified look. The shelf unit stores both dining and office essentials and the long dining table provides work space. Shutting the doors on the compact work station hides office paraphernalia from view without having to pack it away.

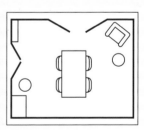

glamour and glitz

This dining area is open to the kitchen, but the use of pattern and colour makes it a sophisticated spot to entertain, especially when the curtains are drawn in the evening. The cabinet beside the window keeps china and cutlery close to hand and a mobile side table means food can be wheeled in from the kitchen.

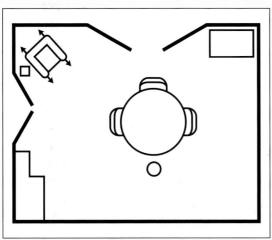

family time

A variety of seating makes this family dining room as flexible as possible. The circular table seats plenty of guests in comfort; extra stools provide more seating, and take up less room at the table than chairs. A rocking chair adds a note of comfort, and is perfect for mums and babies, while a child-sized seat at a low counter makes space for painting.

ONE CONSERVATORY, THREE WAYS

A conservatory is a versatile extra room. The additional space is used for entertaining and relaxing, and simultaneously links your home with your garden.

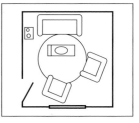

a place in the sun

This conservatory is used as a place to relax in the sunshine with friends. Wicker furniture is a practical choice for conservatories as it doesn't fade in the sunshine. The pinoleum blinds are designed to filter sunshine and cut glare. The sofas and chairs are grouped around the coffee table to enable guests to chat easily.

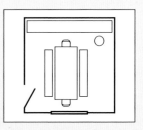

fresh and modern

A conservatory is a great location for a dining room. The modern oak furniture has simple lines and leaves space to allow guests to mingle easily. The built-in window seat means there's room to seat more guests in comfort, while the space beneath is used for storing dining essentials.

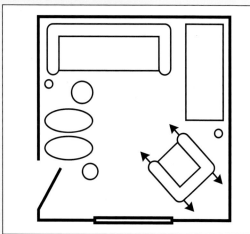

time out

Teenagers and adults alike will love this dedicated space to relax. The deep, comfy sofa was chosen to be large enough to stretch out on with a good book and low enough not to obscure the view of the garden. Beanbags and floor cushions are perfect for lounging and chatting to friends; they are covered in weatherproof fabrics, so they can also be used in the garden.

ONE BEDROOM, THREE WAYS

Decorating the master bedroom can mean devising a room scheme that pleases both partners. These three bedrooms may inspire you.

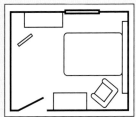

cool and collected

A fuss-free room layout and décor ensures the bedroom always looks calming and inviting. The simple white furniture has been chosen to emphasize the room's feeling of spaciousness, and this is enhanced by the neat blind and freestanding mirror, which brings extra daylight into the room as well as being a very practical piece of furniture.

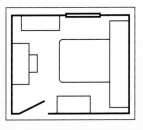

subtle florals

The long storage unit behind the bed provides bedside units on either side of the bed, each with plenty of drawer space, and a shelf behind the headboard for reading lights. A deep panel of graphic floral fabric stitched to the bottom of the curtains introduces colour and pattern without overwhelming the restrained scheme.

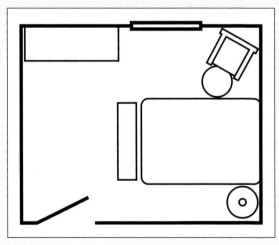

sophisticated glamour

Avoid cluttering the room with too
many pieces of furniture. One
wardrobe plus an extra bench at
the foot of the bed provides
plenty of storage space. A mix of
shimmering fabrics dresses the
bed, with the patterned wallpaper
adding a touch of glamour.

ONE HOME OFFICE, THREE WAYS

A home office doesn't need to be dull. Choose one of these three looks to create a working space you won't want to leave at the end of the day.

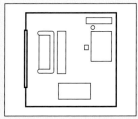

foldaway office

Mobile and foldaway furniture is the perfect solution for a home office where the space needs to be flexible. The tall storage unit is on castors, so it can be wheeled out of the way when not in use, and the computer and desk are housed together in a mobile workstation, with a door that can shut to hide the area from view.

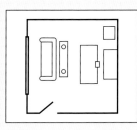

a room of one's own

Office furniture doesn't have to be utilitarian or rather masculine. White-painted wooden furniture creates a home-office area with an elegant, feminine look without being frilly. The tall cupboard and the pretty box files on the console table take care of storage, and the simple writing table has been placed against the wall to encourage quiet concentration.

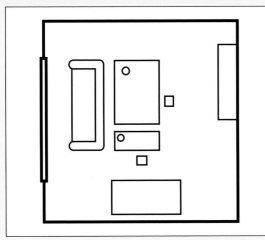

space for two

Finding room for two people to work means careful organization of space. A two-surface, split-level desk means there's plenty of space for two to work in comfort. Modern desk chairs add a fashionable yet practical touch, while wall-mounted storage is perfect for housing small essentials, such as CDs and stationery.

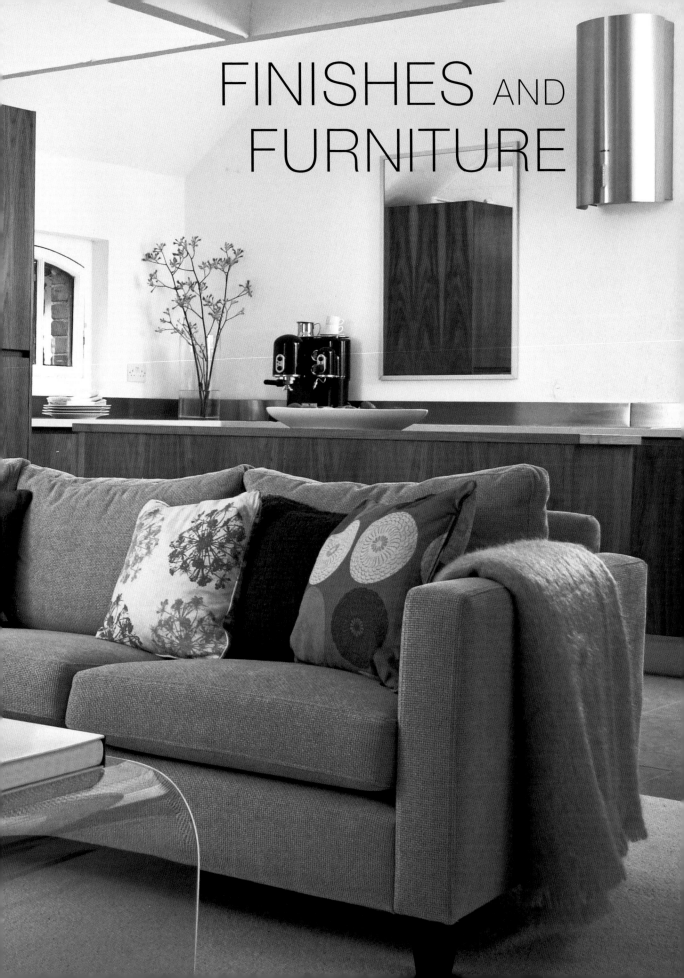

FINISHES AND FURNITURE

MATERIALS

The materials you choose to decorate with have a character all of their own. Whether you're choosing from man-made materials or working with natural products, it's important you choose a material that's suitable for the job.

USING TEXTURE

Together with colour and pattern, texture plays a major part in any decorative scheme. Some materials, such as wood or wool, will have a warm or naturally textured finish that feels good to touch, while others, such as glass and metal, are often smooth and shiny. They add a contemporary element to rooms, and their reflective surfaces help rooms appear larger.

Materials with a glossy or smooth finish bring a sense of luxury, glamour and crispness to a scheme, and because they reflect light they can help a room appear larger than it is. Coarse-textured materials tend to have a natural appeal and their tactile qualities are relaxing and comforting. Soft finishes also help absorb noise and so are good to use in bedrooms, sitting rooms and playrooms.

The texture of the material itself may dictate where you use it in your home. Smooth, man-made surfaces are easy to clean, so are perfect for bathrooms and kitchens, while sumptuous wool throws and pretty voile curtains are better kept out of harm's way in bedrooms.

Glossy or reflective materials include:

- metals
- gloss paint
- mirrors and mirrored furniture
- leather
- metallic wallpapers
- glass
- satin
- silk

Coarse-textured materials include:

- natural flooring
- stone flooring
- terracotta tiles
- wool carpets
- chenille and wool upholstery fabrics
- linens

This cosy spot is created by decorating with several layers of textured soft furnishings. Softly draping curtains, woolly throws, and accessories such as wicker baskets all combine to create a soft, enveloping atmosphere.

LEFT This contemporary
dining room is filled with
light-reflecting materials, from
the glass and chrome dining
table and metal chairs to the
modern-style fireplace and the
mirrors above.

RIGHT Here, fabrics and flooring
in similar colours but with
different textures are combined
to create an interesting scheme
for a day room.

FLOORS

Your floor is constantly walked on, so, as well as being pleasing to look at, your choice needs to be appropriate for the room. Flooring can be used to provide background colour and texture, helping to anchor and balance a decorative scheme.

WOOD

Wooden floors suit both traditional and contemporary interiors, bringing warmth and charm to both styles. The best timbers for flooring include oak, maple, ash and beech. Most modern wooden flooring is made from tongue-and-groove boards which, when laid, help prevent draughts.

Because of the range of shades of natural wood and of the glazes available to seal timber boards, it's possible to find a wooden floor that suits almost every colour scheme. Pale wood shades such as ash and beech help lighten the room, while darker tones create a warm, cosy look. If you would like the floor to have an established look, choose an oiled finish rather than a glossy varnish. In period properties it may be possible to sand the original wooden floorboards, which can then be painted or stained to hide any blemishes and to suit the room's décor.

SOLID WOOD OR LAMINATE?

New wooden floors range widely in style and price. A solid wood floor, made from boards or blocks of a specific hardwood, is a big investment, so if the budget does not stretch to this consider engineered boards or laminate wood flooring, which are man-made alternatives designed to resemble solid wood. Once installed they can look indistinguishable from a solid wood floor.

Engineered boards, also known as multi-layered boards, are a high-quality alternative to solid wood, and are made from several layers of one hardwood.

Laminate flooring is a wood-effect flooring, and the many products available vary wildly in quality and longevity. It is usually constructed from a thin sliver of hardwood veneer pasted on to a board, which is made from an inexpensive wood alternative such as plywood. Some inexpensive laminates use an image of the wood printed on to paper rather than a hardwood veneer.

Reclaimed flooring is another readily available wood flooring option and many antique boards have a wonderful patina. You may need to sand and/or seal the floorboards once they have been installed.

Whichever style you choose, the new wooden floor will need to be laid across the existing sub-floor. Allow the floor to acclimatize to the room before it is laid. The installation cost will vary according to the nature of the wood, the style of flooring, and whether you need the boards to be stained or sealed once they are in situ.

Insider info

You can also get the look of an exotic hardwood floor by choosing unsealed boards made from a less expensive hardwood such as oak. Then stain the boards with a coloured, protective woodstain; this will darken the colour of the wood while letting the grain show through. If you don't fancy the task yourself, many flooring installers will stain wooden boards to order, prior to installation.

RIGHT Slate tiles are an inexpensive way of using natural stone in the home. Slate comes in a range of shades, but the most usual colour for slate tiles is charcoal grey.

OPPOSITE Laminate wooden flooring in a warm shade of cherry brings some rich colour to this conservatory. The floor's easy-to-clean surface is a practical choice as the room is also a thoroughfare out to the garden.

STONE

Quarried for centuries all over the world, and the flooring of choice in our most venerable buildings, stone floors develop a patina with age which only improves their natural good looks.

Limestone, sandstone and slate are the most commonly used stones, together giving a choice of shades from creamy whites, yellows and greens right through to the darkest black, and including interesting natural textures and patterning.

Hard-wearing and long-lasting, stone floors are another investment buy. For a more inexpensive option,

go for slate tiles or reproduction stones, which are designed to resemble ancient flagstones but come without the accompanying price tag. Reclaimed stone tiles or flagstones are another option.

Always choose a professional installer to lay a stone floor. You will need to discuss your floor's suitability for stone with the installer before you buy, as heavy stone slabs should be laid on a concrete sub-floor. If you are looking for stone flooring for an upstairs room, or you live in an apartment that's several floors up, you should choose stone tiles because they are thinner and lighter than flagstones.

TILES

Tiles for floors vary widely in size, style and shape, from colourful porcelain tiles with textured finishes to rustic terracotta squares and delicate mosaic tiles. Hard-wearing and waterproof, floor tiles are a good choice for bathrooms and kitchens and some suit heavy-traffic areas such as hallways.

Contemporary large-scale porcelain tiles are becoming popular for family rooms such as kitchen/dining rooms, living rooms and conservatories. They can also be used to add a designer touch to floors, and contemporary ranges include tiles designed to resemble leather, or tiles filled with tiny diamante sparkle – ideal for adding the wow factor to bathrooms or shower-rooms.

Quick trick

Most terracotta tiles need to be sealed once laid to ensure they are waterproof. Instead, go for pre-sealed terracotta tiles to save yourself time.

With their large dimensions and glossy looks, contemporary porcelain tiles are a great choice for modern kitchens, and because they're easy to clean and long lasting they're also a practical option.

LEFT Traditional encaustic tiles, in a range of earthy shades, bring colour and pattern to this hallway floor. The colour goes all the way through these clay-based tiles, so will never wear away.

BELOW Inexpensive, waterproof and non-slip, vinyl tiles are safe and practical for wet areas such as bathrooms.

OTHER TYPES OF HARD FLOORING

There are plenty of man-made and natural varieties of hard flooring to choose from.

VINYL

Vinyl flooring ranges in style from inexpensive tiles to top-quality vinyl that's designed to resemble natural materials such as stone. It comes in sheets or ready-cut squares, and can be a good budget choice.

LINOLEUM

A natural product made from a mix of ingredients that includes ground limestone and linseed oil, lino is a hard-wearing and versatile hard flooring which comes in a good choice of colours and is enjoying a revival. It can be laid in various ways, either as sheet flooring or as tiles. Clever installers can create bespoke patterns or interesting chequerboard-effect floors.

CONCRETE

A new concrete floor requires sealing to make it water-resistant, and it can also be painted with specialist concrete paint to make it fit in with the rest of the room's scheme. Alternatively, polishing a concrete floor to a high-gloss finish adds a modern look to the room.

RUBBER

Available in a huge range of colours and textured finishes, rubber flooring is also highly practical: it's hard-wearing, non-slip and easy to clean. Perfect for kids' playrooms, it also suits kitchens and bathrooms.

CORK

Soft and warm underfoot, cork tiles are porous and must be sealed before use. Cork tiles come in natural colours, or laminated with photographic images.

If you'd like to fill your walls with colour, use a plain carpet to balance the scheme. Here, the pale carpet is a neutral backdrop to the citrus brightness of the walls, soft furnishings and accessories.

Quick trick

If you don't want to go to the expense and hassle of fitting wall-to-wall carpets, consider laying rugs. Many flooring companies also make large rugs; order a size that covers most of the floor space and you've got an instant room update that you can take with you when you move.

CARPET

Wall-to-wall fitted carpets have timeless appeal. They are soft and warm underfoot and therefore perfect for draughty floors or bedrooms.

As carpets are chosen to last, ensure you're buying the right carpet for your home. 100 per cent wool carpets are a luxurious choice that suit lighter-traffic areas such as dining rooms, bedrooms and sitting rooms. For busier areas, with a lot of toing and froing, such as hallways and stairs, the more standard 80 per cent wool/20 per cent nylon mix is harder wearing and will last longer.

The majority of carpets are either woven or tufted. Woven carpets are more labour intensive to manufacture than tufted carpets, and this is reflected in their price. The two classic weaves are Axminster and Wilton, which are ways of manufacture, not brand names. Axminster carpets usually have patterns woven into the carpets, while Wilton carpets tend to be plain but can include up to five different shades. A tufted carpet will be of high enough quality to suit our twenty-first-century homes.

Carpets also come in several textured finishes ranging from smooth velvet piles to twist and loop piles, which have a rougher, more informal look. You might also like an uncut loop, which gives carpet a more natural woven look (see page 115) and has no pile.

When buying a new carpet, also replace the existing underlay as new underlay will prolong the life of your carpet – over-extending the life of old underlay is a false economy, as is doing without underlay altogether. Remember to include the price of underlay and installation in the price of the carpet, to get a true reflection of the finished cost. Unless you're very good at DIY, it's advisable to pay for carpet installation to be done by a professional.

RUGS

Rugs and runners are an excellent way to bring colour and pattern to your floors. Flat-weave rugs with geometric patterns or cheerful colours are a good choice for hallways or children's bedrooms, and kilims and dhurries imported from Asia or inexpensive washable cotton rugs are all an instant way to add splashes of bright colour to any floor.

Rug-making is an ancient craft, and antique rugs are expensive treasures, but their traditional patterns are still made today. Contemporary designer rugs have become an art form, and are currently extremely popular, with the most sought after considered an investment purchase. Many are designed with bold patterns, a textural finish or interesting colour combinations which ensure the rug will be the room's focal point. If this is the case with the rug you choose, keep the rest of the room's décor calm and unfussy, to avoid any pattern or colour clashes.

There is a huge variety of rugs available, so think carefully about the style and size of the rug before you buy. Measure the available floor space and think about how much of the floor you would like the rug to cover. Bear in mind that rugs play visual tricks on our eyes and can make the floor space in a large room appear smaller, which can be a benefit if you'd like the room to appear more cosy.

STAIR CARPET

In all but the most grand or contemporary homes, the staircase will have been designed to be covered. In practice, this means you have a choice between carpet or natural flooring. Short-pile carpets are a good option as they are easier to clean (the pile does not trap as much dust as longer-pile versions), and a wool/nylon mix is more suitable for stairs than a 100 per cent pure wool carpet as it is harder wearing. Natural flooring can look wonderful, but ask about the suitability for stairs. Some types, such as seagrass and jute, are not recommended as they can be either too slippery or not tough enough to withstand the constant use.

A good-looking option which suits both traditional and modern interiors is a woven stair runner made from natural flooring or carpet. These usually come in several standard widths to fit most stairs, and are bought by the length required to fit your staircase. As with standard carpet, all stair carpets should be professionally fitted.

Hard-wearing traditional carpet in a practical shade such as this blue/grey is the perfect flooring for stairs.

NATURAL FLOORING

Sisal, seagrass, coir, jute, rush and paper are the most common forms of natural flooring. Each comes from natural, renewable sources such as grasses and the leaves of plants, and paper flooring is derived from wood pulp. These sources ensure that natural flooring is an environmentally friendly option for the ecologically aware consumer. They come in a range of natural, neutral shades and are woven into different finishes, textures and patterns that suit both contemporary and traditional interiors.

Each natural flooring material has its own character, so ensure you choose the right one for your room.

Jute is soft underfoot and suits bedrooms.

Durable, inexpensive **coir** is tough on bare feet but a good choice for hallways and conservatories.

Versatile **sisal** can be used in most rooms of the house, and comes in the widest range of shades, weaves and textures.

LEFT It's now possible to find natural flooring dyed in deep shades, such as this eye-catching navy-blue sisal floor covering. Use it in place of traditional carpet to give your floor colour and texture.

ABOVE Neutral in tone and with a textured finish, natural flooring provides a perfect background colour for a room that's decorated in muted shades of cream and pale blue.

Seagrass comes in a range of interesting weaves, and can be used in most areas, apart from the stairs.

Paper is hard-wearing and has a crisp, contemporary look. It can be used in most areas apart from the stairs.

Traditional **rush matting** is one of the few natural floorings that's suitable for bathrooms, as it benefits from the damp atmosphere.

Bamboo is another type of natural flooring, but unlike the soft variations mentioned above, which are considered alternatives to carpet, it is one of the hardest natural materials available for flooring, and so is a good alternative to natural wood boards. Like other natural floorings it can be an environmentally sound choice, as it is a sustainable resource – bamboo's fast growth means that the canes can be harvested within five years of planting.

Whatever type you choose, remember that all natural flooring needs 48 hours to acclimatize to your home's environment before it is laid.

MIX AND MATCH

If you like the look of natural flooring but would prefer to lay a carpet, go for a wool or wool-mix carpet with a loop pile. Alternatively, choose a carpet that's a mix of wool and natural flooring.

A natural rug brings comfort, softness and texture to this tiled sitting room floor.

Insider info

The textured finish of natural flooring can make it hard to mop up spillages. If you're concerned about stains, the flooring can be treated with an environmentally friendly stain-resistant solution, which is applied to the flooring when it is cut.

WALLS

What you put on your walls will play a large part in determining the overall look of your finished room. From shimmering papers to chalky emulsion paints, the huge variety available ensures every room will look unique.

PAINT

Paint is a wonderful way to instantly transform your walls. Inexpensive, easy for the amateur to accomplish, and available in an infinite variety of shades, it's the simplest and quickest way to make a decorative stamp on your home.

TYPES OF PAINT FOR WALLS

Emulsion is a water-based paint used on the main body of interior walls. Matt emulsion, which dries to a flat, non-reflective finish, is the most popular. Silk emulsion, which dries to a slight sheen, is hard-wearing and wipeable. Both come in a huge range of colours.

Gloss and **eggshell** paints are usually applied to interior woodwork and metalwork. Both are available as traditional oil-based paints but also as water-based

formulations, which are low-odour and fast-drying. Gloss, as its name suggests, dries to a high gloss finish, while eggshell has a low-sheen finish.

Specialist **kitchen/bathroom paints** are designed to resist moisture. They are a good choice for rooms with high humidity, and some contain a fungicide to cope with damp conditions.

Traditional paints are made to historic recipes, and include old-fashioned paints such as **limewash** and **distemper**, as well as those which dry to an ultra-matt or chalky finish. **Ecological paints** are also made to traditional recipes and include little or no environmentally unfriendly ingredients (see box). Both are likely to be made with natural pigments. These paints often have high 'breathability' and may suit older buildings where the walls need to breathe. Always check with the paint manufacturer before using these paints, as both the walls and the paint may need special preparation. Planning a painted decorative scheme usually involves choosing one colour for the walls and another for all the woodwork and the ceiling, so the room looks coordinated and balanced. Many stores offer a paint-mixing service, so that water-based paints can be mixed to a very specific colour, and even computer-matched to a colour in a fabric, for example. For information on DIY painting, see Your Design Scheme.

Paints and the environment

Conventional paints contain volatile organic compounds (VOCs) which are released into the environment and contribute to atmospheric pollution. Manufacturers are working to produce paints with low odour and low VOCs, and paints are graded according to an industry-wide system. So check the label before you buy; in general, water-based paints have a lower VOC content than oil-based paints.

LEFT Paint for walls comes in a huge range of colours, from pale pastel shades to dramatic dark ones, such as this deep grey. Teamed with white-painted woodwork, white furniture and a white carpet to lift the scheme, the charcoal-grey walls ensure that this home office looks striking and contemporary.

RIGHT In low-ceilinged attic rooms, painting the walls and ceiling in the same white shade helps the room appear more spacious, light and airy.

OPPOSITE If the walls to be painted are in a humid environment such as a bathroom, opt for a specialist paint that is designed to cope with damp conditions.

LEFT Large floral patterned wallpaper is a great choice for bedrooms. Here it is used to create an accent wall, highlighting the headboard and shelf above.

BELOW Two-tone papers in muted shades bring gentle pattern and colour to a room, as seen in this living space.

WALLPAPER

Wallpaper has shaken off its conventional image and now comes in an awe-inspiring selection of designs, from large-scale patterns that hark back to traditional motifs, to glossy metallic finishes that bring a sense of glamour to the walls. Stripes, florals, textured papers, metals, plains and bold patterns such as damasks all add their own individual look to a room.

Creating an accent wall is a perfect way to start decorating with wallpaper. Because you're not covering the walls of an entire room you can choose a more expensive paper than the budget might otherwise allow. A large-scale pattern is perfect for this treatment and adds a designer touch to rooms such as bedrooms and dining rooms. Wallpaper featuring large-scale digital images – either of landscapes or family snaps – also looks very effective when hung in this way.

Wallpapers vary in quality from top-of-the-range hand-blocked papers produced using traditional methods to inexpensive mass-produced designs. As hanging wallpaper requires more skill than painting, it may be worth employing a professional, especially if you have chosen an expensive design.

TILES

Wall tiles are a practical choice for bathrooms, shower-rooms and kitchen splashbacks. They range from mass-produced patterned budget choices through to hand-crafted glazed tiles with individual patterns, porcelain tiles designed to look like wood or with leather-effect finishes, translucent coloured glass tiles and metallic tiles in shades from bronze to gold.

The vast array of sizes and styles mean the colour and pattern that tiles can bring to a wall are almost unlimited. You can build up your own designs using a patchwork effect of different plain tiles, individualize a tiled wall with a contrasting border or interesting single tiles, perhaps in glass, to punctuate a plain expanse, or cover the walls with delicate geometric mosaic tiles.

Standard ceramic wall tiles can be square or rectangular. Square tiles range from 10 x 10 cm (4 x 4 in) to 13 x 13 cm (5 x 5 in) depending on their manufacturer. Rectangular tiles range from 7.5 x 15 cm (3 x 6 in) to 10 x 20 cm (4 x 8 in). In recent years, large-scale porcelain tiles have become popular as a covering for walls. These are larger (usually around 30 x 60 cm) than standard ceramic tiles and their large size and interesting textural finishes, such as marble and granite effects, give a modern twist to walls in kitchens and bathrooms.

ABOVE In this bathroom plain white tiles are combined with tiny mosaic tiles in bright shades of blue to bring colour and pattern to the walls.

RIGHT Varying the sizes of the tiles on the wall creates a tiled area with a sense of movement and interest. The tiles' textured finish also brings a subtle pattern to the area.

ALTERNATIVES FOR WALLS

Don't feel constrained by wallpaper and paint. There are other materials to help make your home unique.

BRICK

Exposed brickwork can either add a rustic look or have a highly contemporary appeal. Reclaimed bricks can be found at salvage yards and can be used to clad existing interior walls in older houses, while modern brickwork in new properties can be left exposed to add a sense of loft-style living to the scheme.

WOOD PANELLING

Wood panelling is ideal for covering uneven plastering or wall surfaces while giving walls a uniform look that can be easily painted to coordinate with the room's décor. Tongue-and-groove panelling made from inexpensive softwood is ideal for giving rooms a country-cottage or beach-house look, especially when painted white or a muted neutral shade. Modern timber

panelling, which ranges from varnished sheets of wood veneer to expensive hardwood slatted panels, may suit contemporary homes.

GLASS

Glass lets in light and helps small spaces seem larger. Other than for windows, using glass as a structural material is almost always associated with contemporary homes. New technology means glass can now be used as room partitions, external walls and even as flooring. Get expert advice from glass manufacturers on which type you will need for your project.

METAL

Sheet metal used as splashbacks on walls or as flooring gives homes an urban, industrial and contemporary look. Stainless steel and aluminium are the most commonly used metals, often chosen for kitchens to mimic the style of professional chef's kitchens.

LEFT Glass is a popular choice for contemporary fitted kitchens and its smooth, light-reflecting surface makes it an ideal material for a splashback, as seen here.

ABOVE Leaving the brickwork exposed gives the stairwell in this home a rough-textured yet appealing surface. The adjacent wall has been covered with wood panelling to disguise the uneven surface and to hide pipes and electric cables.

Quick ideas to refresh your home

Take a good look at what's on your walls and floors already; a freshen up may mean you don't need to redecorate completely.

Carpets: get carpets and natural flooring professionally cleaned; a three-bedroom house will only take a couple of hours to clean. This can result in a dramatic change in the look of the floor.

Bathroom tiles: clean grout with bleach, or remove old grout with a screwdriver then re-grout with new plain white grout, for tiles that will look as good as new.

Floors: if your budget won't stretch to new flooring, lift up the carpet and see what's beneath. Existing floorboards can be repaired and sanded by professional companies; or, if you're keen, hire a sanding machine and do the job yourself. Concrete sub-floors can be cleaned, then painted and varnished.

Painted walls: painted walls can get dirty, especially in hallways and kitchens. Wash the walls gently with a sugar-soap solution to remove grease, grime and dirty fingerprints. Sugar soap is used to clean walls prior to painting, and you may find that a simple wash is all you need to get painted walls looking as good as new.

Woodwork: windowsills, skirtings and, in older properties, picture and dado rails all attract dust. Clean them, and if need be sand lightly then update with a new coat of eggshell or gloss paint to disguise knocks and chipped areas.

Freshly painted walls make an entrance hall seem instantly inviting and welcoming.

THE FINISHED LOOK

A successful room scheme needs to contain contrasts to be visually stimulating. Too much of one material in a room will mean there's not enough contrast, but too many and the room will simply look muddled. Here's some helpful guidance through all the possibilities.

finishes and furniture

Some materials have a natural affinity with each other:
☐ Wood and stone go well together. Go for stone floors and wooden worktops in a kitchen; in bathrooms combine wooden washstands with stone tiles on the floor and walls.
☐ Patterned wallpaper and neutral carpet is a classic combination that suits dining rooms, bedrooms and sitting rooms.
☐ Stone tiles and chunky sheets of glass work together well in bathrooms; a glass basin or thick shower screen together with large-scale, tactile stone tiles on the walls creates a sumptuous bathroom.

RIGHT A mix of ingredients creates a bathroom that's full of visual interest, from the smooth china basins and chunky wooden washstand surface to the contrasting styles of cream and dark green wall tiles.

Use two different materials as a visual signal of a change in the room's purpose or to emphasize the texture of each:
☐ In an open-plan kitchen/diner, laying a wood floor or carpet in the dining area and vinyl in the kitchen is a practical way to distinguish between the two areas.
☐ An instant way to add textural contrast is to place rugs on the floor. In the hallway or sitting room, colourful and inexpensive kilim rugs will jazz up laminate flooring, while in the bedroom a shaggy sheepskin rug placed over carpet feels glorious under bare feet.

LEFT Mixing smooth granite surfaces with shiny metal units and an aluminium Venetian blind gives this kitchen contemporary appeal.

KEY STYLE FEATURES

There's a variety of materials in this sitting room, but the simple colour scheme gives the room a unified look.

The cream cotton upholstery of the armchair contrasts with the leather sofa both in fabric choice and colourway.

The smooth laminate floor is softened with the addition of a soft cream rug.

Wicker baskets add their own open texture, in contrast to the smoothness of the china ornaments.

The leather on the sofa shines with a subtle sheen. Cotton and linen cushions and a woolly textural throw provide a tactile contrast.

FURNITURE

From the scrubbed kitchen table that you've owned for years to your favourite armchair in front of the television, whatever its style, provenance or age, your furniture turns a house into your home.

Most of us can't afford to replace every piece of furniture each time we change our décor. Instead, breathe new life into your rooms with a rethink about the furniture you own; you may be pleasantly surprised about the changes you can engineer without spending any money at all.

DO A FURNITURE AUDIT

Doing a furniture audit forces you to be matter-of-fact about what you own and whether you want – or need – to keep it.

Questions to ask yourself about your furniture:

1 Is it useful?
2 Do I like it?
3 If my budget could stretch to it, would I replace it?
4 Is there a home for it somewhere else in the house?

If the furniture is no longer wanted, get rid of it to avoid filling your home with clutter. Some furniture companies will remove old pieces of furniture as part of their delivery service, while local authorities may offer junk-removal services. Another option is to find out whether there are any free recycling schemes in place in your area.

RESITE YOUR FURNITURE

Use Question 4 in the audit above to help you think laterally about your furniture.

If you'd like to replace your bed, can it be moved to a guest room? If your child has outgrown bunk beds, would a younger sibling love to inherit them? Can an old single bed become a day bed in a playroom or family room?

LEFT Re-upholstering favourite pieces of furniture, like this comfy armchair, is a great way to give existing furniture a new lease of life.

If it's time to invest in a new sofa, can you move the old sofa to a bedroom? Teenagers love bedrooms that double as bed-sitting rooms. Consider new upholstery for old armchairs, or move them to guest bedrooms, bathrooms or even landings; with a bookshelf beside a comfy chair you can create a quiet reading area.

Can dining chairs be re-upholstered in a more fashionable fabric to give them a new lease of life? If not, can they become kitchen chairs or office chairs?

Small occasional tables such as sitting-room side tables, lamp tables and butler's trays are equally useful as bedside tables. Old bookshelves can be used to create a home-office space in a corner of a guest room, or a homework area in a child's bedroom.

OPPOSITE Dual-purpose furniture, such as day beds and ottomans, is ideal for rooms that double up as home offices and great bedrooms.

RIGHT Garden tables don't need to stay outside: this pretty wire-work table makes an excellent bedside table.

GIVE YOUR FURNITURE A NEW LOOK

If you're certain you can't move the furniture elsewhere, then it may be possible to give it a fresh new look. A different headboard gives a divan bed a completely new look for the fraction of the cost of a new bed. There are many options available, from painted wood for a Scandinavian look to rattan for an ethnic feel.

A new sofa in a sitting room completely rejuvenates the look of a room, but could the existing sofa or chairs be re-upholstered in a fabric to coordinate with the colours of the new scheme?

Fitted furniture, such as bath panels, bookshelves and kitchen cupboards, is easily updated with a coat of paint. Handles on cabinets, internal doors, and kitchen cupboards and drawers are easily replaced. Try crystal or brass handles for a traditional look; colourful resin or sleek chrome for a more modern interior.

Insider info

While cheap and cheerful kitchen tables and dining chairs are a wonderful way to equip your home inexpensively, don't scrimp on major pieces such as mattresses and sofas. Your bed and sofa are where you relax, and so they should be as comfortable as possible. See pages 128 and 132.

The framework of sofas and armchairs lasts much longer than the covers. Many companies offer a re-upholstering service, and will also revive or replace sagging seat cushions, enabling you to give a new lease of life to furniture that's just tired, not at the end of its life.

BELOW Simple cube shelving, such as this basic wall-mounted unit, is perfect for providing storage and display space in smaller rooms.

CHOOSING FURNITURE FOR YOUR HOME

Whether you're heading for a department store or the local antiques centre, the rules of furniture shopping are the same. Before you buy, consider:

☐ What do you actually need?

☐ What's your budget?

☐ How do you use the room?

☐ Are you looking for an investment piece, or an inexpensive item that doesn't need to stand the test of time?

Thinking in advance about budget and practical issues means you're less likely to make an expensive mistake. It can be as basic as choosing washable loose covers on sofas in family homes, or opting for folding or mobile furniture if space at home is limited.

If you need more information on how to choose furniture that fits your rooms, turn to Assess your Space. If you're not sure what style of furniture you like, check out the Style section in Style and Colour.

BELOW It's good to have surfaces for cups, glasses or books within easy reach of wherever people are sitting, but too many side tables can get in the way much of the time. A nest of tables provides convenience without clutter.

SPACE-SAVING AND DUAL-USE FURNITURE

When space is tight, choose furniture that is foldable, mobile or has more than one use. Furniture on castors can be wheeled out of the way to make more room for living; consider castors on beds, office storage units and kitchen islands.

A sofa bed in a playroom or sitting room means a spare bed for guests. Futon mattresses are easy to produce as overnight beds, and can then be rolled up and stored in a cupboard when not needed. Alternatively, go for a futon mattress with a simple wooden slatted base which lies flat as a bed and folds in half to become a sofa during the day.

A folding, gate-leg or extending table can be used half open on a daily basis, but can be fully opened when entertaining. Folding dining chairs are easily stored out of the way when they're not needed. A home-office desk can double up as a dressing table in a guest bedroom, while the filing can be hidden from view in storage ottomans.

FURNITURE FOR SITTING ROOMS

In living rooms, mix comfy seating with plenty of surfaces to create a room for relaxing and entertaining. Group sofas and armchairs together for a convivial and welcoming arrangement, and include side tables and shelving for storage and display.

In most sitting rooms, the sofa is the largest and most dominant piece of furniture. Three-seater sofas are rarely sat on by three people and traditional three-piece suites take up a lot of space. Instead, consider buying two smaller two-seater sofas that seat four. Place them opposite each other with a coffee table in between to create a convivial arrangement. Modular sofas suit modern sitting rooms and are flexible enough to seat plenty of guests. Think about the upholstery; leather and washable covers are ideal for family sitting rooms, while luxurious velvets and damasks suit rooms that don't need to stand up to too much wear and tear.

Surfaces are essential for cups, glasses, lamps and ornaments. A coffee table is useful and should be low enough not to interrupt the flow of the conversation across it. A nest of tables means extra side tables are available for guests, but can be stored out of the way.

ABOVE Low-level storage that doubles as extra seating is a great option for family living rooms.

RIGHT With their light structure and simple, modern shapes, clear Perspex side and coffee tables are ideal for contemporary sitting rooms.

KEY STYLE FEATURES

Mixing leather and wood furniture creates a cosy sitting room with modern neutral shades of cream and brown.

Leather upholstery is more practical than it appears. It lasts for years, developing a rich patina as it wears, and it's also simple to wipe clean and so is suitable for families.

The coffee table has plenty of space for coffee cups and glasses, and the drawers beneath keep games and magazines close to hand.

A console table, placed in the window, provides extra shelf space for books, flowers and ornaments.

FURNITURE FOR DINING ROOMS

If you love to entertain, a dining area is a must, whether it's in a dedicated room or sharing space with a kitchen or living room. Whatever the size of the space available, you will need a table, chairs and some storage space.

Consider a folding, gate-leg or extending table if space is tight and you rarely entertain more than six people at once. Family dining spaces need a table that's easy to clean; this is not the place for valuable antiques. Go for a modern table with a wipeable surface or a table made from unfinished wood which can be scrubbed clean and occasionally oiled to preserve the wood.

Upholstered dining chairs look wonderful in grand dining rooms or in dining areas which are part of a sitting room. In kitchen/diners go for a more informal look; wooden benches, modern stacking chairs, and metal or wooden folding garden chairs have a relaxed feel and take up little space. Storage for dinnerware is essential. A traditional dresser is ideal for a dedicated dining room, while purpose-built cupboards suit kitchen/diners.

BELOW A simple wooden kitchen table, with a pair of benches as seating, is an understated furniture choice that suits the dining area of a spacious kitchen.

LEFT A central kitchen island is also the dining table in this contemporary kitchen. The folding chairs are easily moved when the island surface is needed for food preparation and the tall cupboards provide ample storage space for dinnerware and glasses as well as kitchen essentials.

KEY STYLE FEATURES

Classic wood furniture and a warm colour palette make this dining room a welcoming space for entertaining.

A console table at the back of the room stores dinnerware, and the extra surface can be used for serving food.

This plain and solid timber dining table is neither too formal nor informal, and sets the right note for many different types of meals.

Mixing and matching different styles of chairs – here wooden chairs are placed alongside upholstered ones – adds an informal touch.

FURNITURE FOR BEDROOMS

Keep bedrooms calm and relaxing, with a decent-sized bed, and free of clutter. Some pieces for storing clothes such as a wardrobe and chest of drawers, plus a bedside table or two, are other elements you may need to include.

If you're buying a new bed, buy the largest bed you can afford and which will fit the space, especially if you share your bed with a partner. A large bed usually means a better night's sleep. Test new mattresses in store to ensure they're comfortable.

Changing the headboard on a divan bed can alter the look of the whole room, as can investing in an entirely new bedstead. Beds come in a huge variety of styles, from ornate metalwork to historical sleigh beds or contemporary streamlined designs.

If you'd love a separate dressing room or walk-in closet but don't have the space, consider fitting built-in wardrobes. Custom-built designs include plenty of hanging space plus shelves for folded clothes and dedicated space for ties, shoes and bags.

ABOVE Cream-painted wrought-iron bedsteads have a romantic air. A small circular occasional table, used as a bedside table, keeps night-time essentials within reach.

LEFT Choosing a four-poster bed has immediately added character to this bedroom, but the streamlined wooden frame means it doesn't overwhelm, and dressing the bed frame with delicate fabrics adds to the romantic appeal. A pair of simple wooden bedside tables nicely complements the wooden bed frame.

KEY STYLE FEATURES

This off-white painted furniture is a classic choice for bedrooms and provides a balance to the pink floral prints.

A cream linen headboard smartens up a basic divan bed. With pale fabric headboards such as these, ensure the fabric can be removed so it can be washed or dry-cleaned.

A slimline console table at the end of the bed is ideal for keeping magazines and books within easy reach.

The chest of drawers doubles up as a bedside table; this is a good option if space is tight in your bedroom.

Placing a bench seat in the window draws attention to the window recess.

FURNITURE FOR HOME OFFICES

Most of us need space at home to undertake personal administration, while for many home is also our place of work. The furniture you need will depend on how often you use the space and where the office is situated within your home.

DESKS AND CHAIRS

For short stretches doing routine paperwork or for occasional bouts of desk work, any convenient table and chair can double as work chair and desk, but if you are a desk-bound home worker you should invest in a proper office chair. It should be height-adjustable, and support your back, to allow you to write or type for extended periods without strain.

When it comes to a desk, think what sort of work surface you require. A desk is essentially just a table, but it doesn't have to be wooden and rectangular; look out for round ones, glass-topped ones and acrylic ones in funky colours. You may be lucky enough to be able to dedicate a room solely as an office, but, if your home office has to share space in another room, consider how a dining table might double as a desk, or a pretty table could become either a desk or a bedroom dressing table, as required. Another space-saving alternative is a fold-down table.

BELOW Office furniture can also be classic and chic, as this white painted desk with its coordinating chair and open bookshelves demonstrate.

ABOVE An upholstered ottoman that opens to reveal space for hanging files is the perfect solution for a home office that doubles as part of a living area.

If you will be working with a screen and keyboard, consider a dedicated computer desk that incorporates a pull-out keyboard shelf, plus storage for discs and other computer essentials. If you're sharing your office space with another room, a good option is a purpose-built home-office unit that closes neatly, hiding everything inside it, when work is finished for the day. Alternatively, go for a mobile work station which can be wheeled to one side when not in use.

STORAGE

Allow for plenty of accessible storage. Traditional options include a desk with its own integrated filing drawers or a stand-alone filing cabinet, while wall-mounted cube shelving provides contemporary storage that suits modern home offices. If the office is also a living room or bedroom, choose furniture that suits both purposes. Bookshelves can house box files unobtrusively and an upholstered ottoman is the ideal place to store files discreetly in bedrooms. In guest rooms, small cabinet-style bedside tables can also hide paperwork from view.

KEY STYLE FEATURES

Tucking the home-office area into part of the sitting room calls for furniture which matches the room's decorative scheme.

The bureau has a traditional shape that suits this sitting room, but has plenty of space for desk work.

The noticeboard keeps notes and cards accessible.

A tall shelving unit stores filing and other paperwork.

WINDOW TREATMENTS

The way the windows are treated has a big influence on the finished look of a room. Curtains, blinds and shutters all aid a room's privacy, dress the window, and alter the amount of natural light that can enter the room.

CURTAINS

Curtains are the most popular form of window dressing chosen for our living spaces. We love them for their practical uses – they aid the room's privacy and help keep it warm and draught-free – but, more importantly, we choose them because they help influence the atmosphere and style of the room. Whatever the curtain style, the softness and drape of the folds of hanging fabric brings a cosy, comforting element to our homes.

ASSESSING YOUR WINDOWS

Before you think about fabrics and curtain headings, take a look at the window itself. Study the window shape, its size and its relation to the rest of the room. Bear in mind the architectural style of the room as a whole; casement windows in a low-ceilinged cottage need a completely different window treatment from a large bay window in a Victorian home. Aim for the curtains to work with the proportions of the room.

Think about the amount of light which comes into the room, and whether you'd like to take advantage of this, or if you need curtains that help to darken the room for sleep.

CURTAIN KNOW-HOW

Large, bulky curtains make small windows look over-dressed, while floor-length curtains help to make rooms appear taller. Maximize the amount of sunshine in darker rooms by ensuring the curtains pull right back from the window. Long, wide curtains – such as those needed for bay windows – are a great way to show off a fabric with a large-scale or dramatic pattern. These days window treatments tend to be understated with few flounces or pelmets, whatever the age of the house or style of interior.

CHOOSING CURTAIN LENGTH

The standard lengths for curtains are sill-length, below the sill, and floor-length.

Floor-length curtains make a definite design statement, drawing the eye to the window whether the curtains are pulled or drawn. They use a substantial amount of fabric and are therefore more expensive to make or to buy.

Sill- and below-sill-length curtains are less costly to make or to buy, as they use less fabric. They are less formal, and can add a 'country-cottage' effect to windows. They suit smaller windows or windows in small rooms where floor-length curtains would look much too grand.

Picking curtains in the same shade as the walls helps rooms to appear larger, as it's harder to see where the walls end and the window begins. These simple tie-top curtains have been customized with a deep border of contrasting blue fabric to coordinate with the rest of the room's colour scheme.

KEY STYLE FEATURES

Together, the curtains and blinds maintain the light, fresh feel of the bay window in this sitting room.

Long sheer curtains have a sophisticated look, and their length and colour soften the lines of the large window.

Roller blinds filter the daylight which shines into the room. A soft shade of pink means the light takes on a rosy hue, which warms up the off-white décor.

CURTAIN FABRICS

The range of fabrics on sale can be baffling, and so having some ideas in your head about the look you want to create will help narrow down your choice. Consider your budget and the style of the rest of the room. Is it large and formal? Simple and contemporary? Small and cosy? What kind of effect do you want: soft and romantic, crisp and modern, dramatic? Compare your chosen swatches with the paint or wallpaper swatches to ensure the elements work together.

Tip

For patterned curtains that aren't too expensive and are reasonably hard-wearing, go for a printed cotton, linen or cotton/linen mix.

Floor-length apple-green curtains bring a splash of fresh springtime colour to this sitting room.

Sheer panels and unlined curtains or heavy drapes and lined curtains

Why choose sheer panels and unlined curtains?

- They're easy and inexpensive to make or buy.
- They filter light into the room, softening direct sunlight, which is ideal if you need privacy during the day but don't wish to exclude the daylight from entering the room.
- Unlined curtains can be washed, which is not advised for lined curtains as the two fabrics could shrink at different rates.
- You can have two sets, so you can hang one set while the other is being washed, or choose a set in a different shade to vary the look of the room.
- A small, inexpensive curtain pole is all you need to suspend them from the window.

Why choose heavy drapes, lined and interlined curtains?

- The extra layer of lining fabric and, on interlined curtains, the interlining padding will keep draughts at bay, and help the room feel warm and cosy.
- They can help the window and room look grand and luxurious. Linked and intertwined curtains drape well when hung.
- Thick or multi-layered fabrics help dampen echoes within the room, and muffle noise from the street outside.
- Linings protect curtain fabric, so it lasts longer and doesn't fade.
- Choose a beautiful pole and elegant finials to hang the curtains to create a window treatment with style and panache.

A sheer curtain with a pretty scalloped edge is hung alongside a heavier pair of curtains to lend this bedroom a romantic, feminine air.

FOR SHEER PANELS, CHOOSE FROM:

Cotton: lightweight cotton, plain or embroidered with a delicate design, makes pretty curtains which help filter light in sunny rooms.

Voile: made from cotton, linen or man-made fibres, voile can be plain or printed with a subtle pattern. Very light and sheer, voile is often used as an alternative to old-fashioned net curtains.

FOR PLAIN CURTAINS, CHOOSE FROM:

Linen and linen union (a cotton/linen mix): linen hangs well and comes in an almost limitless number of colours.

Cotton: versatile cotton comes in an extensive range of grades and colours. Cotton twill, a pure cotton fabric with an interesting weave, is a good choice for plain curtains.

Calico: this inexpensive plain cotton fabric comes in a natural shade that suits neutral room décor.

FOR GLAMOROUS CURTAINS, CHOOSE FROM:

Velvet: available in a great variety of colours and patterns, velvet curtains look elegant and luxurious.

Silk: pure, natural silk comes in a huge range of colours and patterns. Shot silk, woven from threads in two different colours, is a popular choice for luxury curtains.

Damask: made from cotton, man-made fabrics or silk, damask has a woven pattern in two tones of the same shade. Damask curtains have a grand look that suits classic rooms.

FOR PATTERNED CURTAINS, CHOOSE FROM:

Printed patterns: from toile de Jouy, printed with pictorial scenes, to graphic retro patterns, there's an amazing variety of prints available. Floral prints are perennially popular.

Woven patterns: with these, the pattern is woven into the fabric, rather than printed on the surface. Designs include woven stripes, ethnic weaves and damasks. Checked fabric is a popular weave, and the options range from sombre tartans to pretty, diminutive two-tone ginghams.

HANGING YOUR CURTAINS

Curtains are usually hung at the windows from a pole or a track. Tracks, made from metal or plastic, are useful for windows where there is little space between the top of the window and the ceiling, and for bay windows, as they can be bent to fit with the curves of the window. Tracks are not as aesthetically pleasing to look at as poles and, while this isn't a problem when the curtains are drawn, the track will be visible during the day when the curtains are pulled back, unless concealed by some form of pelmet.

Curtain poles come in a huge range of styles and designs. Usually made from wood or metal, poles suit curtains with contemporary headings such as tab-top, tie-top and eyelets, as well as traditionally headed curtains which hang from the pole from coordinating rings. Ensure the pole you are buying is strong enough to support your curtains, as long interlined curtains are extremely heavy. Decorative finials, in glass, metal, wood or resin, fixed to each end of the pole, can be chosen to coordinate with your room scheme.

Curtain poles and tracks should be fitted so they are longer than the length of the window. This means you can pull the curtains right back to frame the window, and let in as much daylight as possible.

ABOVE Smart vertical-striped curtains and a coordinating inner roller blind help to dramatize this sash window. Finishing the curtains with eyelets, rather than a traditional pleat heading, adds a contemporary touch to the window treatment.

LEFT Delicate, floaty sheers make ideal curtains for informal rooms, filtering the sunshine as it comes into the room.

Get the look for less

Choose an inexpensive curtain pole – DIY stores usually have a good selection of basic poles in various widths – then glam it up with a pair of exotic finials. You will get the look of a custom-made designer pole without the expense.

CURTAIN HEADINGS

Your choice of heading will determine the final look of the window. Simple, lightweight curtains can have an unobtrusive standard heading, which is created by pulling a heading tape by hand. Heavier curtains require a more substantial finish, such as box pleats or triple pleats, which are sewn into the curtains when they are made and add a formal air to the finished curtains.

Other alternatives include tab-top curtains, where the curtains are hung from the pole with loops made from the same or contrasting fabric. These tabs can also be concealed, so the pole is not visible, or sometimes tied around the pole for an informal look (often known as tie-tops).

Eyelets are metal rings that are punched into the curtains when they are made, and are a modern method of hanging curtains. They make the curtains extremely easy to hang, and give the finished window treatment a contemporary look.

RIGHT A combination of eyelet headings and a simple metal pole ensure this window treatment looks modern and fresh. Simple metal finials complete the look.

Curtain clips are an instant way to hang curtains. They clip on to the fabric and hang from the rings on the pole, but are only suitable for hanging lightweight, unlined curtains such as sheer voile panels.

CURTAIN LININGS

There are various ways of lining curtains. For loose-lined curtains, the lining fabric is sewn to the top and sides but not the base of the curtain fabric. This is the easiest way to line curtains. For locked-in lined curtains, the lining fabric is sewn on to the reverse of the curtain to give it a more substantial, heavy feel. Interlined curtains have a layer of padding inserted between the lining fabric and the curtain fabric. The curtain is then thicker, hangs well, keeps out draughts, and looks well-made and luxurious. Curtains can be lined with detachable curtain linings. Blackout linings are ideal for rooms where the morning sun could disturb sleepers, or for children's bedrooms.

LEFT Hanging two sets of curtains at a window adds pattern and colour. The sheer curtains filter sunshine during the day, while the heavier cotton print curtains make the room cosy at night.

BLINDS AND SHUTTERS

Blinds are a simpler window treatment than curtains. They can be made from upholstery fabrics, or from a wide range of other materials including wood, metal and plastic. They are often a good solution for wet areas such as kitchens and bathrooms, and frequently suit contemporary living spaces.

Roller blinds work on a simple mechanism which takes up little space at the top of the window recess, and are usually made from stiffened fabric. They can also be made as pull-up blinds, where the roller action is fitted to the base of the window, and the blind pulls up to hide the lower part of the window from view. Large-scale roller blinds are also available; printed with a photographic image or a dramatic pattern, they add colour and interest to a large window without the need for curtains.

Roman blinds concertina in a series of folds to the top of the window recess. They can be made in a variety of fabrics and look particularly smart made from quality linens. They suit bedrooms and living rooms, and give rooms a smart look without being fussy.

Venetian blinds have tiltable, horizontal slats, usually made from wood or metal, which can filter the light into the room while the blind is down. They are good for home offices as they remove glare from workspaces or computer screens, and they also fit contemporary kitchens and bathrooms.

BELOW LEFT Roman blinds can be hung inside the window recess or, as here, outside it. The neutral tones and subtle pattern of the blind's fabric help create a calming atmosphere.

ABOVE A Venetian blind in dark wood is an eye-catching yet simple contemporary window treatment.

BELOW A simple roller blind, made from woven wood, is understated yet modern.

Modern louvred shutters are a great choice for kitchens. They are easy to clean, unlike fabric curtains and blinds, and so will cope with splashes. Keeping the shutters pulled across the windows, but opening the slats, means that sunlight can filter into the room.

SHUTTERS

Shutters, whether traditional panelled designs or modern louvred versions made with tiltable horizontal wooden slats, are an alternative to curtains and blinds. Modern shutters are often a popular choice in urban areas, as the shutters can be kept folded across windows and doors to maintain privacy, but the slats can be opened to let fresh air and sunshine into the room. Whatever the style, shutters keep rooms completely dark at night-time, which helps to aid restful sleep.

Shutters can be made to fit almost any window shape and so are a good option for awkward windows where you can't fit curtains. Whatever the shape of the window, you will need to ensure that there's enough wall space on either side for the shutters to fold back.

Quick trick

If you love the look of unlined, floaty curtains in bedrooms but can't sleep unless the room is dark, fix simple roller blinds made from blackout fabric to the inside of the window recess. Your windows will still have a dreamy, ethereal look but you will avoid the early-morning waking.

LIGHTING

By successfully combining several different types of lighting you will be able to layer the lights, turning some on and others off, according to how you're using the room and the atmosphere you want to create.

TYPES OF ROOM LIGHTING

A successful scheme includes a mix of four different types of lighting.

Ambient lighting: sometimes referred to as general or background lighting, this is the light we see by. It's provided by the sun through windows, and at night by a mix of artificial lights, such as pendant lights, wall lights and floor lights.

Task lighting: This is directional lighting which lights our work. It can include desk lamps, reading lamps and downlighters in a kitchen.

Accent lighting: also known as display lighting, accent lighting is used to highlight interesting objects or architectural details, or in the garden to draw attention to plants.

Decorative lighting: extra lighting, such as strings of lights, candles or a fire, enhance a room's atmosphere.

For living spaces such as bedrooms, dining rooms and sitting rooms, you will use a mix of table, wall, floor and pendant lights. General points to remember are:
☐ always shade the light bulb to avoid glare
☐ vary the heights of the lights in the room; mix wall, table, floor and ceiling lights
☐ position any task lights so you aren't working in your own shadow.

Insider info

Dimmer switches are invaluable for enhancing a room's mood. Replace standard wall switches with dimmer switches; it's a tiny alteration that makes a huge difference to any room's overall appeal.

Clip-on spotlights can be used all around the home as their directional beam makes them ideal as task lights for working at a desk or for reading in bed. They also make inexpensive accent lights: here, clipping the light to the shelf above means it illuminates the display below.

KEY STYLE FEATURES

Choose the right light fitting from wall to ceiling to create the perfect lighting scheme.

Choosing decorative ceiling and wall lights with glass elements helps to bring extra sparkle to the room.

Table lamps help rooms feel cosy. They cast a circular pool of light which creates contrasts between the lit and unlit areas.

Make the most of a pendant light fitting in dining rooms, sitting rooms and hallways by choosing a dramatic design or a decorative shade.

Floor lights are versatile – they can act as reading lamps placed behind armchairs, or shine directional light on to pictures or ornaments.

LIGHTING ROOM BY ROOM

Each room has different lighting requirements, from task lighting to work by to accent lighting that highlights displays and pictures. Considering the different ways in which you use the room will help you decide what's needed.

KITCHENS AND DINING ROOMS

Here you need good task lighting to prepare food by, ambient light for daytime and evening mealtimes, and decorative light if you use the room as a dining room in the evening.

Downlighters installed in the ceiling or under wall-mounted units provide good directional light for food preparation. In the dining area, combine wall lights with a rise-and-fall pendant light to provide ambient light at mealtimes. Candles on the table add atmospheric decorative light. Put all lights on dimmer switches so the level of light in each part of the room can be altered depending on what activity, from cooking to homework, is taking place.

RIGHT A glass chandelier brings romance and elegance to a dining room, and the glass droplets catch the light and help the room sparkle.

LEFT Wall-mounted reading lights are ideal for reading in bed and they also leave space free on bedside tables.

BEDROOMS

Bedrooms need lights to dress by, soft lighting to provide a relaxing mood, and lights to read by in bed. Downlighters in the ceiling, especially near wardrobes or the dressing area, provide light to dress by. Bedside table lamps add soft ambient light and can be easily switched off from the bed. Keen readers can fit reading lights on the wall near the bedhead.

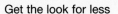

Get the look for less
Give your walls a discreet designer touch by replacing standard white wall switches with chrome, wood or Perspex designs.

RIGHT Placing a floor lamp behind a sofa provides task lighting for reading or sewing when the daylight has faded.

BELOW Illuminating bathroom shelves ensures that all the toiletries and make-up stored here are easily visible and quick to find.

LIVING ROOMS

Living rooms need to feel welcoming and provide a relaxing atmosphere. They usually fulfil many roles, so you will need to think about how to light for different activities, from watching TV to reading and entertaining. Mix table lamps with floor, wall and pendant lights to provide plenty of ambient light. Wall or floor lights can be directional, illuminating interesting architectural details or a spot in which to read. A fire is ideal for atmospheric, decorative light.

BATHROOMS

Task lighting is needed here, for shaving and applying make-up, plus ambient light for day-to-day use. Mood lighting helps the room become a relaxing haven. Soften the bathroom's hard surfaces with well-chosen lighting. Fit wall-mounted lights either side of the mirror, and ensure the ceiling lights are dimmable to add atmosphere. Some bathroom cabinets or mirrors come with built-in lights. There are strict rules regarding lighting in bathrooms, so speak to a qualified electrician before planning your scheme.

BRIGHT IDEAS
SWATCH SELECTOR

Choosing and combining materials to create a room scheme can seem an overwhelming task, whether you're looking for products for walls, floors or window treatments. Take a look at these classic examples of paint, wallpaper, flooring, tiles and fabrics to find inspiration for your room schemes, and check out the Winning Combinations on pages 162–167 to find a mix of swatches that work well together.

WALLS

Your walls are the largest surface to be decorated within your rooms, so what you choose to cover them with will have a huge impact on the finished look. From blocks of solid paint to intricately patterned wallpaper, or a mix of the two, get inspiration from these swatches.

Midway between blue and green, this bright shade of aqua is a lively colour that helps rooms appear larger. Mix it with off-whites and deep chocolate browns.

Apple green is vibrant and fresh, and works well in both modern and older homes.

Pale blue is a perennially popular shade for bedrooms, as it is calming and easy to live with.

A mix of stone and soft green, this subtle paint shade mixes well with colourful patterned fabrics.

Grey-green is a muted shade that suits rooms with plenty of natural sunlight, such as kitchens and conservatories.

A neutral shade of biscuit-coloured paint will bring subtle warmth and colour to walls.

Spring-fresh paint in a citrus yellow will bring sunshine into any room, and is great for livening up kitchens, hallways and playrooms.

Naturally tranquil, lavender is an ideal shade for bedrooms. Combine the paint with silvers, greys and pinks to create a sumptuous look.

Red-painted walls are dramatic yet cosy, and can help dark rooms with little natural light appear warm and appealing.

A deep blue works well on the walls of a large bathroom, especially if it is balanced by well-painted white woodwork.

Creamy pink shades on walls are easy to live with. Mix with natural flooring such as seagrass for a modern take on a country scheme.

Red berry is a warming choice for walls. Ideal for dining rooms, it can also work well in smaller rooms that are used for entertaining, as the rich colour adds cosiness to the space.

Walls with a hint of pink and lilac help bring gentle warm colour into bedrooms. Mix with whites and greys to keep the scheme adult and welcoming rather than girly.

Dark, rich colours such as this chocolate brown should be used with confidence. If using the colour on every wall, ensure the rest of the décor is light and bright, and hang mirrors and light-coloured prints on the walls around the room.

This matt, delicately textured wallpaper is highlighted with soft pin-stripes of dulled silver which sensitively catches the light.

A broad-striped wallpaper can bring a sense of grandeur and order to larger rooms such as living rooms or hallways.

With a subtle pattern and an off-white shade, this versatile wallpaper combines well with patterned carpets or curtains.

Traditional papers with large-scale motifs can add a sense of grandeur to walls.

The large-scale pattern of this wallpaper has a natural, organic feel to it, adding a sense of movement to walls.

Geometric large-scale patterned wallpapers have retro appeal, and used with confidence they can be a talking point in today's living rooms.

These stripes with a textured finish are reminiscent of natural flooring, and would bring an ethnic look to walls.

A flowing pattern is a good choice for walls. Neutral shades of cream, beige and brown fill the walls with unobtrusive warm colour.

Subtle stripes in soft lilacs are an easy-to-live-with pattern choice.

The tonal patterning of this fabric-look wallpaper is subtle yet visible, and mixes well with silk or cotton floral curtains.

Elegant and contemporary, this exotic pattern suits glamorous bedrooms and dining rooms.

A floral sprigged wallpaper is a must for lovers of traditional country style.

Inspired by 18th century chinoiserie, this highly patterned paper will make a bold statement.

Shades of glazed tiles create a wall filled with jewel shades of blue and green. Perfect for a bathroom, this look also suits kitchen splashbacks.

Blue and white patterned Delft-style tiles are a classic look and suit both traditional and modern styles.

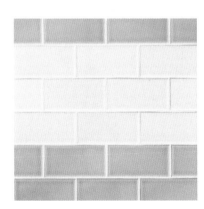

Traditional rectangular tiles – known as elongated tiles – have a utilitarian charm. Mix with standard square tiles to create a border, or use them to cover an entire wall.

Mosaics such as these Roman-inspired tiles add a classic touch to even the smallest shower-room.

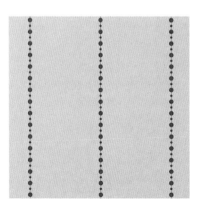

This beaded-stripe wallpaper would make a stunning backdrop in a contemporary dining area.

FLOORS

Changing the flooring can make a dramatic difference to the overall look of a room. As well as looking good it needs to be a practical choice for the room, so take inspiration from our selection of swatches.

Geometric stone mosaic tiles suit both walls and floors in bathrooms.

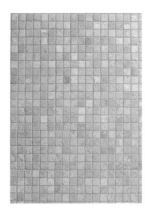

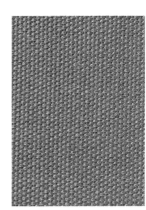

Sisal flooring has a naturally deep toffee shade. Hard-wearing and durable, sisal suits hallways, living rooms and stairs.

With its warm tones and softly textured finish, jute flooring is perfect for master and guest bedrooms.

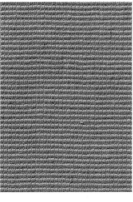

The rich red tones of dark cherry wooden flooring brings warmth to dining rooms and sitting rooms.

This carpet mimics the textured weaves of natural flooring, but is soft underfoot. Its neutral shade means it suits most living spaces.

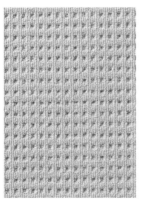

Terracotta tiles come in a suprising variety of shades. Lay them in kitchens and hallways for a floor with traditional, rustic appeal.

Antique oak is one of the most popular types of wooden floors. Warm in tone, it works in both traditional and contemporary living and dining rooms.

Attractive and hard-wearing, oak flooring suits most types of homes and interior styles.

Choosing coir with a herringbone weave draws attention to the natural texture of the coir.

Pale resin flooring, being translucent and glass-like, absorbs colours used in the rest of the décor, yet is hard-wearing and a practical choice for bathrooms.

Carpets made from 100 per cent wool are soft underfoot. This shade is neutral yet warm, suiting bedrooms and living areas.

Off-white floor paint is ideal for wooden floors, instantly adding a country-cottage appeal to bedrooms, hallways and landings.

Laminate wooden flooring can be hard to tell from the real thing. Dark shades don't have to be sombre; team with pale walls and modern furniture for a contemporary and practical look.

Carpet in muted berry tones brings warmth and cosiness to floors. Perfect for bedrooms, team with oyster pink, pale purple, silver and grey for a room that's calm, soothing and relaxing.

Add glamour with hard flooring that has a subtle sparkle. A soft lilac shade adds a pretty, feminine touch to bathrooms.

Deep blue carpets suit living rooms and bedrooms. Mix with fabrics and wallpapers in tones of grey, lilac and blue.

Grey-toned carpets are a practical yet attractive choice for hallways, especially when combined with pale walls and light wood furniture.

This blue/grey shade of rubber flooring will mix well with pale blue and bright scarlet.

With its grey hues and seemingly textured appearance, this linoleum has been designed to resemble stone flooring.

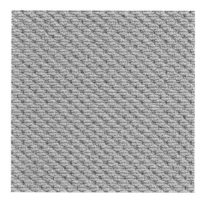

This canvas-coloured woven carpet is easy to live with and suits most rooms; it will coordinate with both neutral and colourful room schemes.

Mosaic tiles bring colour to bathroom and kitchen walls and floors. Combine different coloured tiles for a cheerful surface.

Pale carpets with a simple textured weave provide perfect background colour and subtle texture in sitting rooms and bedrooms.

The weave of this seagrass is simple yet eye-catching and works well in both modern and traditional homes.

Vinyl flooring that is designed to resemble natural wood with a weathered finish is a practical choice for busy rooms.

Slate tiles are ideal for kitchen or hallway floors, where they add a distinguished look. A slate floor is an investment which should last for years.

Clay tiles in a natural shade of pale blue will bring a traditional yet delicate look to floors.

Linoleum flooring in cool shades, designed to look like textured slate, is a great choice for bathrooms.

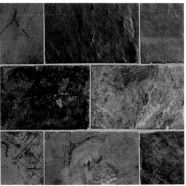

Slate flooring can be shot through with other colours, such as ochre and rust, and is perfect for both urban and country kitchens.

Choose linoleum in wonderful shades of deep ocean blue for a bathroom floor that's both dramatic in colour and a practical choice for a wet area.

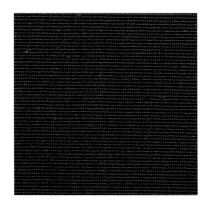

Sisal is a natural flooring which dyes well. Team it with chunky wooden furniture and plain white textured fabrics for a modern room scheme.

Natural floorings are great for many rooms in the house, giving a warm, comforting feel underfoot.

A pearlescent covering underfoot lifts any room and is great in a bathroom or contemporary kitchen.

FABRICS

Fabrics bring colour, pattern and textural softness to a room's scheme. From curtains to upholstery, cushions and throws, choose a selection of different fabrics to create a unique scheme that's bursting with contrast and visual interest.

The deep blue and rough texture of dark denim make it a great choice for upholstery. Team with natural flooring such as coir for a living room.

Large-scale patterns are ideal for curtains in open-plan or large rooms.

A bold-striped fabric introduces colour and geometric pattern.

This modern floral pattern will bring a lively injection of colour and pattern into a room.

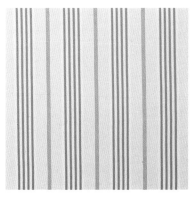

A multi-striped fabric in blue and cream is ideal for creating a beach-house style.

A deep blue fabric with a delicate motif will be perfect for both bedrooms and bathrooms.

A large-scale two-tone floral fabric in shades of blue and off-white lends a classical air to bedrooms.

Classic prints look charming and bring colour and pattern into a room. Avoid overkill by keeping walls and floors plain.

Bold stripes in a selection of bright colours look modern and smart.

Traditional floral prints are perennially popular and suit classic and country-style interiors. Mix with toning ginghams, plains or checks.

A printed floral fabric is ideal for those who love traditional country style. Mix it with stone-coloured carpets and pale apple-green walls.

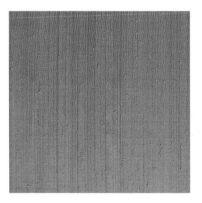

Silk is glamorous and luxurious. Choose it in soft shades of dark taupe or mushroom for an elegant look for curtains and cushions.

Traditional gingham fabrics are synonymous with country-style interiors. They mix well with floral prints chosen in coordinating shades.

Large painterly florals are a classic fabric design. Pick them in bold shades of orange and yellow for a modern window treatment.

Good-quality plain cottons are great for contrasting with more striking patterns. Use them to cover headboards, pillows and chairs.

Fabrics with patterning in their texture, such as this waffle fabric, add interest to plain materials and are ideal for bedlinen.

Fabrics with ethnic-style prints add a dramatic pattern.

Toile de Jouy is a pictorial, two-tone fabric. It's a good choice for bedroom curtains if you like a traditional country look.

Velvet is one of the most sumptuous decorating fabrics. Use it in deep shades, such as scarlet, for long curtains in dining rooms.

Bold contemporary prints have a charm that's hard to beat. This fabric by Marimekko looks great as curtains in a contemporary kitchen.

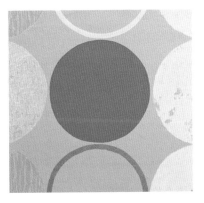

Although grey and orange is an unusual colour combination, it works incredibly well to create a bold, modern look.

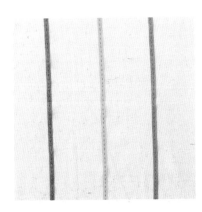

This lively sheer fabric would work well as an internal curtain to hide shelving or wardrobe space.

Sprigged florals are a good way of introducing a delicate pattern into a room. Mix them with coordinating larger-scale florals, checks or stripes.

Woven Jacquard fabrics have a subtle, tonal pattern. A sophisticated choice, they suit curtains and seat covers in sitting and dining rooms.

A printed voile is a good alternative to standard net curtains, filtering light yet maintaining the room's privacy.

Hard-wearing natural linen is a great choice for curtains. Choose a subtle, faded striped fabric for simple yet stylish bedroom curtains.

Soft suede is a luxurious fabric that is ideal for use in the bedroom as a headboard cover or bed throw.

This thin check woollen fabric would be perfect for upholstering chairs and sofas to add a smart clubhouse feel to sitting rooms.

A delicate-patterned fabric in pale blue and gold would suit both contemporary and traditional room schemes.

Although this is a floral fabric, the design has an abstract feel. It would introduce a splash of bright colour without dominating a room.

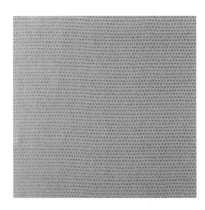

Textured fabrics in colours such as this sage green work well alongside more elaborate floral patterns, helping to provide balance.

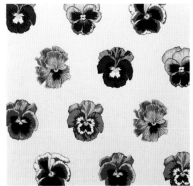

This cheerful pansy print in bright colours is perfect for bringing colour and vibrancy to curtains and cushions in a sitting room.

A deep purple fabric is a dramatic choice for sofa and armchair upholstery. Mix with patterned cushions for contrast.

WINNING COMBINATIONS

COUNTRY CHARM

A floral fabric in blue, green and lilac is the ideal starting point for a traditional bedroom. For a modern take on this look, paint walls in pale apple or pistachio green, and lay textured carpet in pale stone.

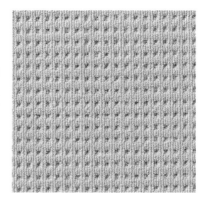

BEACH-HOUSE STYLE

Create a modern scheme for a beach-house-style kitchen by combining striped fabric in shades of bright scarlet and pale blue for blinds and chair covers, together with natural wood flooring and pale walls.

ON THE TILES

For contemporary bathrooms, mosaic tiles are ideal – they bring pattern, colour and fun to walls and are practical for such a wet area. Mix the tiles with painted white walls and rubber flooring.

 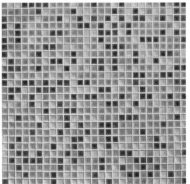 

BRIGHT AND MODERN

Mix large-scale patterns such as this iconic Marimekko print with solid plains, like this rich scarlet, to avoid pattern overkill. Neutral flooring provides the perfect background.

  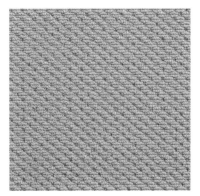

ORIENTAL ACCENT

Hang this ornately patterned wallpaper as an accent wall in a bedroom.
Choose plain, textured curtains, such as silk with a hint of pink. A tactile
carpet in a soft berry shade adds warmth and cosiness.

PURPLE PROSE

This colourful pansy print is great for adding vibrancy; use it for curtains
and cushions, and choose a toning shade of purple to upholster sofas and
armchairs. Pink walls and a seagrass floor anchor the scheme.

  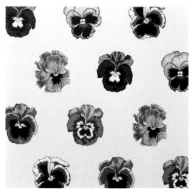

RETRO APPEAL

Large-scale geometric wallpapers work well as a room's focal point. Use the paper on the accent wall and balance it with toning but neutral fabrics and flooring.

FABULOUS FLORALS

Choosing large florals brings a sense of country-style charm to rooms without the pattern looking too small and fussy. Mix with textured woven natural flooring and soft cream painted walls.

COOL AND CLASSIC

Reproduction blue and white Delft tiles look wonderful as accent tiles among plain white tiles on a bathroom wall. Team with off-white painted walls and white curtains and towels. Add warmth with oak-effect laminate floorboards.

NICE AND NEUTRAL

Build up layers of materials in a small palette of neutral shades for a luxurious modern sitting room. The wallpaper's pattern brings life to the walls, silk curtains add glamour and a wool carpet is comforting underfoot.

FRESH AND STYLISH

Mixing stripes and florals in similar shades creates an interesting combination of patterns that can work well in many rooms from bathrooms to bedrooms. Balance with solid plains for walls and floors.

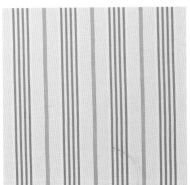

WELL RED

Red is a dramatic and unusual colour for walls. Balance the vibrancy of the walls with a pale carpet and monochrome red and white fabric for curtains, such as this traditional toile de Jouy.

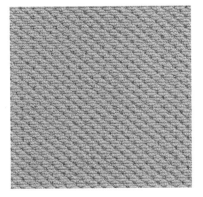

YOUR
DESIGN SCHEME

ORGANIZING YOUR IDEAS

Time spent planning the whole look of the room will pay dividends when the redecoration is finished. Room redesign that is organized in a methodical manner is much more likely to be successful.

GATHERING INFORMATION

If you've got a good understanding of your personal style the decision-making process will be easier; if not, then have a look at the different styles in the Style and Colour chapter (see pages 10–35) to help you narrow down the choices from the different looks available.

Getting inspiration is a key part of the redecoration process. One of the best ways to find inspiration is to look through interiors magazines and home-interest books. Buy them or borrow past issues from your friends, or look online for electronic versions of the magazines – this can be particularly helpful for international editions, which may be difficult to find or expensive to buy. If you can, rip out or print the pictures of rooms that appeal.

Developing your likes and dislikes

When you're looking at your growing collection of images, ask yourself questions:
- Why do I like these rooms?
- Is there a particular atmosphere that my choices have in common?
- Are there any colours, materials, patterns or textures that recur?
- What looks or effects do I actively dislike?

Ideas for design schemes can come from all sorts of sources, such as a piece of statement furniture. This large Chinese cupboard was the starting point for an oriental-inspired sitting room.

Redecorating your sitting room will breathe new life into your home, but ensure you've got a good idea before you begin about how you'd like all the elements – from furniture to carpets, curtains and accessories – to look. This way your room design will come together successfully when you or the decorators have finished.

Begin to group the images together. You can organize them by room types, which makes sense if you're looking for a new look for a particular room. Alternatively, you might find it helpful to group the images by the colourways used, by their overall style, such as ethnic or seaside, or by the mood created by the particular combination of furniture, colours and patterns. By sifting through your collection of images and sorting them into relevant categories you will find you can establish which looks consistently appeal to you and which you definitely want to avoid.

As well as looking at photographs, visit real homes, whether those of your friends or houses open to the public. Think back to places that you've visited, both at home and abroad, and ask yourself what you liked about the look. If you'd like to capture the spirit of somewhere you've stayed, ask yourself why it appealed. Was the house cosy, warm, light, fresh? Was the décor colourful or neutral, the furniture well-loved or glossy and new?

You can also visit design showrooms. They will have fabric and wallpaper books, and large ones may have mocked-up room sets, which can be very helpful in showing how different fabrics and colours combine to create a successful look, and what a particular pattern looks like in different treatments. Flick through sample books and see how the colours and styles of the fabrics and wallpapers work together. Some showrooms may sell to trade only but the staff will still be able to offer you advice, and will tell you where your local stockist is located. Ask for samples of paint, fabric, wallpaper, flooring and trimmings to take away, then file them or pin them up on the wall.

Some showrooms offer interior-design services for a low fee, or a fee which is refundable against a purchase; these can be useful if you're finding it impossible to make up your mind. Ask if the company makes other products, such as accompanying paint or wallpaper ranges, which coordinate with the swatches you've already collected.

ASKING ADVICE

The next stage is to ask advice on materials and items you'd like to use. There's no point setting your heart on something if it's wildly unsuitable for the location you've chosen, or if it will send your project way over budget.

Friends and family can be invaluable. Show them your collection of samples and ask them what they think of your fledgling design scheme. If they have experience of, say, a particular flooring or fabric, ask if they like it and if it has been a success. Unless you live alone and can please yourself, ask the advice of those you share the home with, as they've got to live with the scheme too. Making a few compromises may also reduce the choices, making it easier to choose the final colours, materials and patterns from your initial collection of swatches.

Don't forget the practical issues when considering what material or colour to go for, whether you're planning new floors, walls, curtains or upholstery. It may be possible to cross off several potential products from your list by being realistic about where and when you'd use them. Assess your Space (see page 64) has more information on specific materials and where to use them in your home. Talk to staff in showrooms and

Tip

Buying or borrowing a large fabric or wallpaper sample is particularly important if you're choosing a large-scale pattern, as the small samples given out by design companies rarely give a good impression of what the design will look like when hanging in your home.

department stores too. Their expertise may be helpful, especially if you need advice on the suitability of a particular material, or if you wish to pair one fabric or wallpaper with another. Take up offers of free site visits; seeing a flooring or paint colour you like actually in a real room may reinforce your choice, or change your mind about it.

Build up your design scheme in layers. Choose flooring, a paint colour for the walls and upholstery fabrics, then add decorative details to bring interest and vibrancy to the room.

CHOOSING THE RIGHT COMBINATION

It's the mix of colours and patterns you choose for your room that give it its decorative depth. From your collection of images and swatches you need to choose for your room a workable mix of fabrics, flooring, upholstery and decorative extras.

To begin, pick one material, colour or pattern that will be used throughout the room; it could be wallpaper or paint for the walls, or a wall-to-wall fitted carpet. This will help to anchor and unify the room scheme.

Next bring the scheme to life with contrasts of colour, pattern and texture; it's the layering of these elements which creates decorative interest. In any room, the materials chosen for the furniture, light fittings and curtains, plus their style, will all play a part in how the room comes together as a whole.

Finally add vibrancy and interest with decorative details and finishing touches to bring charm and your personality into the room.

It can seem daunting getting the mix right, so reassure yourself by testing out ideas before you buy.

Think about including space for comfortable seating within an open-plan dining area.

Insider info

Colour shades differ according to the amount of light in a room. Artificial light from standard household bulbs has a yellow tone, and so alters the appearance of some paint and wallpaper shades in the evening. Move the samples around the room so you can see how the light changes throughout the day.

Consider including a separate laundry room or walk-in wardrobe in your plans – they're the new 'must-haves' on many a home-owner's wish list.

Buy sample paint pots of your chosen shades, and paint each one on to a large piece of wallpaper lining paper or thin plywood. Stick these on to the wall and live with the samples for a few days, noticing how the colour alters during daylight and in the evening. Move the sample around the room so you can see how the potential colour looks in different areas of the room.

When choosing fabrics you may be able to request returnable samples, which are larger pieces of fabric, usually a metre or a yard, from design houses (you may have to pay a deposit). If this service isn't available, buy a metre or yard of your favoured fabric. Drape it over the existing sofa or hang it at the window to see how the fabric looks in situ. If it isn't possible to request a large wallpaper sample, consider buying one roll of your chosen paper; you may save yourself money in the long run if you decide the design is not for you. Pin up a large piece of the wallpaper and notice how it looks both during the day and in the evening to ensure you like the pattern, the colourway and the overall effect of the design in your room.

Once your large samples and swatches are hanging in place or are grouped together on a floor, ask yourself some honest questions. Do you like the combination? Is it relaxing, cheerful, comforting, colourful or welcoming enough? Does your partner and do your family like it?

Create your own mood board

Interior designers create a mood board to present their ideas to their clients. They assemble their chosen samples together on one large piece of card to give an impression of how the final scheme will look. If this seems too extreme for you, then it's possible to do a simplified version; simply assemble the samples you like and check that they all work well together. If possible, work with relative sizes of samples; go for a big piece of carpet (the floor is a large part of the room), a smaller piece of upholstery fabric, and a still smaller piece of cushion fabric, for example, so you get an idea of the relationship between the swatches and how they will look when displayed together.

DON'T FORGET THE BUDGET

Working out what you need and how much it's going to cost is not an exciting part of interior decorating, but a very necessary one. You will need to make realistic estimates of materials and labour, or you may be faced with unpleasant surprises along the way.

All design projects need a budget in order to prevent costs escalating. Being aware of how much money you have to spend at the outset will influence your decision-making and ensure you've got enough funds to cover all the work.

Think about what you need to spend the money on. Redoing a bedroom, for example, will need:
☐ flooring
☐ paint or wallpaper, or a mix of the two, for the walls
☐ curtains or other window treatment
☐ perhaps new furniture and bedlinen.
Each of these, except perhaps the paint, can vary wildly in cost and could make or break a budget.

If you've set your heart on a luxurious choice, but the budget won't stretch to it, think laterally. Instead of curtains in fabric you can't afford, perhaps they could be made from an inexpensive fabric with your luxury choice as a border; or go for a blind instead of curtains, which will take much less fabric. Similarly, an expensive wallpaper could be used on only one wall to create an accent.

If there's no way your budget will stretch to a special designer choice, shop around. See if you can find a similar, less expensive product somewhere else. Keep the image or sample with you when shopping. Try DIY stores for lighting ranges which look great and yet cost a fraction of one-off designer pieces, or look at flooring that's designed to resemble marble, stone or wood without the price tag attached.

HIDDEN COSTS

Be careful to take into account any extras you will need to pay for.

Flooring: new carpets need new underlay, and most types of hard flooring require professional installation.

Curtains: the cost will include lining fabric, heading tape, plus a pole or track as well as the actual curtain fabric.

Lighting: most people will have to pay an electrician to install new wall or ceiling lights.

Labour: if you're not doing it yourself you will need to pay for redecorating tasks such as painting, wallpapering and tiling.

Keep kitchen restoration costs down by replacing the unit doors instead of fitting an entirely new kitchen.

The latest look or a lasting look?
Choosing the most fashionable items now may mean your room quickly looks dated. Unless you're prepared to redecorate regularly, opt for good-quality classics that will stand the test of time.

QUANTITIES

Working out how much you need to spend depends largely on the quantities of materials you need. If in doubt, always get an expert to calculate the costs for you to avoid expensive mistakes.

PAINT QUANTITIES

First calculate the area of the surface to be painted. Working *either* in metres or feet, multiply the height of the area by the width. This will give you a figure in square metres (or square feet). There's no need to subtract window or door areas.

As a rough guide, 1 litre of emulsion will cover about 11–13 sq m of internal walls and ceilings. (A gallon of paint will cover about 350 sq ft of internal walls and ceilings.) However, paint coverage varies from brand to brand, so check the label on the can, as this will usually give a coverage estimate.

To work out how much paint you will need, divide the surface area you've calculated by the coverage figure to get the number of litres (or gallons) it will take.

Paint for domestic interiors is sold in standard-sized cans, from 500 ml cans through to huge 5 or even 10 litre cans (or from ¼ pint cans to 1 gallon size). Make sure you buy enough paint for at least one coat, especially if you are having it mixed to order.

Tip

The amount of paint you need will also depend on the existing colour of your walls. You will need more paint to cover a dark colour than a light one.

WALLPAPER QUANTITIES

Wallpaper is sold in rolls, which usually measure 10 m (33 ft) long and 52 cm (21 in) wide. To work out how many rolls to buy, you will need to know how many 'drops' (wall-height lengths) you will get from each roll.

1. Measure the height of the walls, excluding any skirting or coving. Add 10 cm (4 in) to this as an overhang allowance. If your paper has a pattern which needs to be matched, measure the length of the repeat on the paper, and add this length to the wall height as well as the 10 cm (4 in). This figure is the length of paper you will need for each drop. (Wallpaper books give the pattern repeat on their samples, to help you with this calculation.)
Formula: height of walls + 10 cm (4 in) + length of pattern repeat = the length of the drop.

2. To work out how many drops you will get from each roll of wallpaper, divide the total length of the roll by the length of the drop.
Formula: length of roll (usually 10 m/33 ft) ÷ length of drop = how many drops per roll.

Painting the walls is an instant and inexpensive way to bring colour and atmosphere into a bedroom, leaving more of the budget free to be spent on glamorous bedlinen and decorative details such as paintings and prints.

3. Next, measure the width of each wall to be papered, and add these figures together. Divide this by the width of the roll to find out how many drops of wallpaper you will need to paper the area.
Formula: total width of walls ÷ width of roll (usually 52 cm/21 in) = number of drops needed.

4. To arrive at the number of rolls you need to buy, divide the total number of drops you will need by the number of drops you will get from each roll. Round the figure up to a whole number of rolls, then add on an extra one in case of accidents.
Formula: number of drops needed to paper room ÷ number of drops per roll + 1 = number of rolls of wallpaper you need to buy.

If your answer to step 2 is just short of a complete number of drops – say, 3¾ drops – you must discount the part-drop from your calculations (so two rolls will give you 6 complete drops, not 7), but bear in mind that these extra pieces may be suitable for papering shorter areas such as above doors or a fireplace.

If you're choosing a large-scale patterned wallpaper such as this dramatic floral print it can be impossible to judge from a small sample how the completed wall will look. Before committing yourself, buy one roll and hang a length in place to get a better idea of the impact of the pattern and colours.

Tip
Always buy wallpaper from the same batch to ensure colour consistency. You can do this by checking the batch number, which will be printed on the roll.

FLOORING

Carpet and many types of flooring, such as vinyl, lino and laminate wood, are sold by the square metre (or square foot). Using either metres or feet, accurately measure the length and width of your floor and multiply the two together to get the total area you will need.

· Tip

As it is likely you will be using professionals to install new flooring, consider arranging a site visit prior to ordering. They'll be able to advise on the correct floor to choose and ensure the existing sub-floor is suitable for the product.

BELOW Laminate wood flooring is an inexpensive and practical choice for family rooms. If you're adept at DIY you can tackle the installation yourself; otherwise ask your flooring showroom to recommend a local fitter.

TILES

Tiles are sold individually or by the square metre (or square foot). Measure the height and the width of the area to be tiled, and multiply these figures together. This gives the area to be tiled. To find out how many individual tiles you need, divide the area to be tiled by the area of the single tile. Add on 10 per cent of this figure to allow for breakages and wastage.

ABOVE Tiles are ideal for bathroom walls and floors. If you haven't laid them yourself before, start with a small area such as a splashback above the basin.

Tip

Always buy all the tiles you need from the same batch to avoid problems with colour matching. Include some extra tiles just in case you need to replace any broken tiles in the future.

MEASURING UP FOR CURTAINS

Fabrics for curtains and blinds are sold by the metre (or yard). The quantity of fabric you will need will depend not only on your window size but also the style of curtains you'd like and the pattern on the fabric.

To establish how much fabric you will need, you must first measure your window. This is much easier if the pole or track is already in place. If it isn't, you will have to estimate the position of the pole as accurately as you can.

1. Measure the length of the pole or track (not the window). Depending on the heading style you want for the curtains, the fabric width should be at least 1.5 times as wide as the length of the pole or track, and most headings need more. For example, pencil pleats, the most commonly used heading for lined curtains, will take a total fabric width of about 2.5 times the length of the pole.

2. Multiply the length of the pole/track by 2.5 (or whatever your chosen heading requires), then add about 7.5 cm (3 in) per curtain as a seam allowance. Divide this figure by the width of your chosen fabric to get the number of fabric widths you need.

3. Establish how long you want the finished curtains to be: either floor-length or sill-length, for example. Measure from this point to the top of the pole or track. Add a hem and heading allowance of between 15 and 25 cm (6–10 in). This figure is the working length of the curtains. In addition to this you will need to allow extra if the fabric has a repeating pattern (see page 180).

4. Finally, multiply the number of fabric widths by the working length (including pattern repeat allowance) to get the number of metres or yards of fabric you need to buy.

The formula looks like this:

Number of fabric widths required x (working length of the curtains + pattern repeat allowance) = number of metres (or yards) of fabric needed.

Generously made full-length curtains draw attention to the window, framing the view to the outside. Pull them back to the wall so that sunshine can flood into the room.

Let the professionals step in

If you're at all unsure, take your window measurements to the store where the sales assistant can do the calculations for you, based on your chosen fabric. Alternatively, ask a curtain-maker to visit you at home, to measure the window and calculate the fabric quantities required. This way you will be sure the curtains will fit correctly once they're made – if they don't, you will be able to ask them to redress the problem.

LEFT Offcuts of expensive fabrics need not go to waste: use them to make coordinating scatter cushions.

OPPOSITE Simple Roman blinds, made from lightweight cotton, help diffuse sunlight as it enters the room.

ALLOWING FOR THE PATTERN REPEAT

Patterned fabrics have a repeat, which is the distance between the beginning of the pattern to where it starts to repeat further down the same length of fabric. Patterns will need to be matched at all the vertical seams that join fabric widths. They will also need to align across the two separate curtains so that, when the curtains are hanging, the same part of the pattern is at the same level on both of the curtains. In practice, for a small repeat this means buying just a little more fabric than you might have planned on, but a large, bold pattern may take a lot of extra fabric and involve quite a bit of wastage. Staff in the fabric store will help you establish how much fabric you need, but if you're by yourself the easiest way is to measure the repeat on the fabric, then add this amount to your working length measurement.

Tip

If you'd like the curtains to hang below the pole so it can be seen when the curtains are closed, measure from the curtain rings downwards. A track, however, should always be hidden when the curtains are closed.

MEASURING UP FOR BLINDS

Measurements for blinds depend on the style of the blind, and whether you're planning on hanging the blind inside or outside the window recess. Roman blinds, for example, with their attractive but plentiful folds of fabric, require careful calculations.

To measure up for a blind that will be fitted inside the recess, measure the height and width of the window recess. For roller blinds, you will need to deduct 3 cm (1¼ in) from the width measurement for the roller mechanism and add an extra 30 cm (12 in) to the height measurement; this will allow enough fabric for the hem at the bottom and to cover the roller at the top of the blind.

If you'd prefer the blind to hang outside the window recess, measure the length of the window from the point above the window where you will fix the blind's hanging system to the sill at the base of the window (or below, if you'd like a longer blind). Measure the width of the window outside the window recess. If you'd like the blind to hang so that it blocks any light coming into the room, add 10 cm (4 in) to this width measurement.

As the quantity of fabric needed depends on the style of blind, keep these measurements with you when shopping for fabric. You can then ask the assistant to calculate the amount you will need to buy based on your window measurements, the fabric chosen, and the blind design you prefer.

PLANNING THE SCHEME

It helps to organize the order of the work before it begins. When redecorating one room it is relatively straightforward to work out just what should happen when, but large and complex jobs will need careful planning.

AN ORGANIZED APPROACH

Whether large or small, a design project should progress in this order:

Planning: this includes investigating all the options, planning the budget, and then choosing your materials according to aesthetic, practical and financial constraints. Depending on the size of the job, you may want to get advice from or commission architects, builders and in-house designers.

Sourcing materials: this ranges from fabric for curtains to flooring and interior architecture. If you're working on a large project be sure your builders know which materials you want to use, and who will source them.

The work itself: whether it's a DIY job or a complicated house renovation, the work should take place in a logical order. If there are several jobs to be done, consider asking one contractor to take care of all of the stages, rather than hiring several individual firms yourself. This saves time as the workmen are sub-contracted to carry out their work in a coordinated way.

Tip

For your redecoration to be a success, you need to be aware of the amount of space you have available. If you're in doubt as to whether your scheme will suit the space or if you will be able to adapt your existing space to make the new look work, then check out the guidelines in Assess Your Space.

TIMING

All home-improvement projects take time, and it's easy to underestimate how long each job will take. Don't set yourself an unrealistic target to get the job done in time for a particular deadline, such as the holiday season or the arrival of a new baby, as this will just add to your stress levels. Good decorators and builders are usually busy. Once you've found a firm you like, be prepared to wait for them to be able to start on your job. Get a realistic estimate from the contractor as to how long the work will take so you can plan your diary.

If you're doing the job yourself, be realistic about how much time you can spend on the project each evening or weekend. Preparation both at the planning stage and in the room before the work begins, plus the timescale of the work itself, may all take longer than you had originally thought, especially if you're a weekend DIY-er with a full-time job and family to look after.

Custom-built integrated storage, such as this wine rack and shoe holder set in a busy corner of a family kitchen, needs to be considered at the planning stage, but is the sort of detail that makes the most of available space.

The amount of work required to fit a kitchen means that the cabinets and integrated appliances are fitted after the plumbing and electrics but before any redecoration.

ORDER OF WORK: A CHECKLIST

Once you've planned and sourced the materials, work begins. Ensure that the work progresses in a logical way, with any structural alterations taking place before redecoration starts.

For smaller jobs which don't require building work, aim to tackle the tasks in this order:

1. Plumbing: the disruption to your home life when plumbing work is taking place will depend on the nature of the work. If pipework is not being repositioned, a new bath and WC can be installed in a day, but adding a new shower or cloakroom will take much longer. Always ensure the plumbing work is completed before starting redecoration.

2. Electrics: install any new electrical cabling before redecoration work begins. If you're installing ceiling lights the flooring above may have to be taken up.

3. Plastering: if any replastering needs to be done, this should be allowed to dry before redecoration of walls or ceiling begins.

4. Redecorating: do any tiling first, then paint the walls above. When painting, paint walls and ceiling first, then woodwork. Hang wallpaper after tiling or painting jobs are completed.

5. Flooring: when the walls and ceiling are ready, you can lay the new flooring.

6. Furniture: once the walls and floors are redecorated, you can move in freestanding furniture. Aim for deliveries of new furniture to take place after the room has been completed, unless you've got space to store it elsewhere.

7. Pictures and ornaments: art and ornaments are the finishing touches that make the room your own.

Tips

If you're installing new fitted furniture, such as a fitted kitchen, or fitted wardrobes in the bedroom, you may want to wait until this work is done before redecorating or laying new flooring.

If you are fitting lights to illuminate pictures and artwork, you need to have planned by this stage where the lights will be located; this means some advance thought about where the pictures are going to be hanging in the redesigned room.

GET IN THE EXPERTS, OR DIY?

There are plenty of home improvements that can be accomplished by the confident and able amateur, but others take time to learn and some are definitely better left to the experts, as mistakes can be costly to rectify.

Learning some basic DIY skills can save you time and money. Armed with these and an essential tool kit, you will feel confident enough to tackle the easy jobs yourself. Putting up pictures, using a small power drill and putting together flat-pack furniture that comes with instructions are all skills that are easily mastered. While you may feel nervous tackling them initially, with confidence and practice you will get better and better. Don't be afraid to ask advice from friends and family who are more experienced than you are when it comes to home improvements.

Buy or hire?

If you do want to attempt a more complicated task you may find it simpler to hire, rather than buy, large pieces of specialist DIY equipment such as floor sanders and long ladders, especially if you plan only to use them once or if storage at home is limited.

HOME IMPROVEMENT TASKS

JOB: Assembling flat-pack furniture

TASK INVOLVES	Assembling boards with screws, nails, adhesives
SKILL LEVEL	Low
DO IT YOURSELF?	Yes, if confident

JOB: Putting up shelves on walls

TASK INVOLVES	Making secure fittings to walls, fitting shelves to fixings
SKILL LEVEL	Low to Medium
DO IT YOURSELF?	Yes, if confident

JOB: Laying carpet

TASK INVOLVES	Removing existing flooring, laying new underlay, cutting to size and laying new carpet
SKILL LEVEL	High
DO IT YOURSELF?	No. Carpet is expensive, and laying it is complicated; this is a job best left to the professionals

JOB: Hanging a new door

TASK INVOLVES	Screwing hinges to the door frame and door itself, ensuring it hangs straight and opens and closes easily
SKILL LEVEL	Medium
DO IT YOURSELF?	Yes, if confident, although getting a door well balanced can be tricky

JOB: Installing a flat-pack kitchen

TASK INVOLVES	Removing old kitchen, assembling new flat-pack units, connecting water supplies, cutting worktop to fit, among others
SKILL LEVEL	High
DO IT YOURSELF?	No, unless very skilled and patient

JOB: Stripping excess paint from window frames

TASK INVOLVES	Using a power planer or chemical stripper to remove the old paint
SKILL LEVEL	Low to Medium
DO IT YOURSELF?	Yes, if confident

JOB: Fitting window locks

TASK INVOLVES	Screwing ready-made locks to window frames
SKILL LEVEL	Low
DO IT YOURSELF?	Yes, if confident

JOB: Painting interior walls and woodwork

TASK INVOLVES	Preparing surfaces, painting surfaces
SKILL LEVEL	Low to Medium
DO IT YOURSELF?	Yes, if confident

JOB: Hanging wallpaper

TASK INVOLVES	Preparing walls, hanging wallpaper
SKILL LEVEL	Medium, but the difficulty level depends on the room's architecture and the wallpaper chosen
DO IT YOURSELF?	Yes, if confident, but beginners should start with an easy-to-hang paper with a simple pattern

JOB: Sanding floors

TASK INVOLVES	Preparing the floor (possibly removing existing flooring), sealing doors to room, sanding floorboards with an industrial sander, painting or varnishing sanded boards
SKILL LEVEL	Medium to High
DO IT YOURSELF?	Yes, if confident, bearing in mind that it is a very physical job. For speed, employ a professional

JOB: Staining or varnishing wood

TASK INVOLVES	Changing the colour of the wood without obscuring the grain, or varnishing to protect the wood; can be done on furniture, doors and floorboards
SKILL LEVEL	Medium
DO IT YOURSELF?	Yes, but the time needed will depend on the piece of furniture or floor size

JOB: Tiling walls or floors

TASK INVOLVES	Preparing the surface, tiling the surface including cutting tiles to size and finishing the surface with grout and sealant
SKILL LEVEL	Medium to High
DO IT YOURSELF?	Yes, if confident. You may want professional help with large floor tiles or expensive wall tiles over a large area

JOB: Laying laminate wood flooring

TASK INVOLVES	Possibly removing existing flooring, laying new boards, pinning beading in place around skirtings to finish
SKILL LEVEL	Medium
DO IT YOURSELF?	Yes, if confident

JOB: Laying solid wood flooring

TASK INVOLVES	Possibly removing existing flooring, laying new boards
SKILL LEVEL	High
DO IT YOURSELF?	No: solid wood boards are expensive and laying them is a complicated process best left to the professionals

JOB: Sanding down furniture

TASK INVOLVES	Using sandpaper or a power sander to remove old paint and varnish from furniture
SKILL LEVEL	Low to Medium
DO IT YOURSELF?	Yes, if confident

JOB: Putting up curtain tracks and poles, and blinds

TASK INVOLVES	Fixing track, pole and blind fittings to walls
SKILL LEVEL	Low to Medium, depending on the window recess
DO IT YOURSELF?	Yes, if confident. The larger the pole or track, for example around a bay window, the more complicated its fixing, and so if you're not confident you may find it easier and quicker to pay for installation

EMPLOYING PROFESSIONALS

It's important to choose the right people for a job. Not only do you want the work done on time, to budget, and to look how you've planned it, but also a good working relationship will be essential, especially if they're going to be in your home for some time.

FINDING TRADESMEN

To find a tradesman such as a builder or decorator, ask friends and family for recommendations of local firms who have done work on their houses – word of mouth is the best way to find tradesmen you can trust. If this isn't possible, accredited trade organizations often have search facilities for local members in your area. Employing a builder or contractor who's a member of a trade organization should guarantee you workmen of a reasonable level of competence, and you will be able to use the organization's complaints procedure should the job go wrong.

Always get references from previous customers. If a tradesman can't give you contact details of satisfied customers who are happy to talk to you, then ask yourself why. If possible, and this is particularly important for big jobs, go and see the work and ask the householder if the job progressed smoothly and if they're happy with the finished work. Seeing the quality of the work first hand will also give you a better understanding of the quotes when they come in; a low quote may not be the best option if the workmanship is of an unsatisfactory standard. Ask the previous customer what the building or decorating team were like to deal with when they were on site, as you need to know that you will be able to work with them when they are in your home. Questions to ask include: Did they start the job when they said they would? Was the job finished on time? Were they reliable and did they arrive for work at the same time every day? Did the job keep to the agreed budget set out on the quote?

GETTING QUOTES

Once you've found a builder or decorator you believe can do the job for you, it's important to get an accurate quote for the work. Ask three tradesmen or firms for quotes so you get a better idea of the price.

Ensure that you, the customer, know exactly what you want done and that you convey this accurately and fully. It may help to share the ideas you've gleaned from your brainstorming sessions, such as pictures from a magazine or book. Provide a written specification of what you want done, and ask for a written quote which specifies exactly the stages of the work needed and the cost to you; this can include tasks such as tidying up or clearing away after the job itself is completed.

If at any stage you aren't clear about terms or processes, don't be intimidated by the jargon, but ask for a clear explanation. Misunderstandings now may lead to problems when the job is under way.

Changing your mind when the work has begun will naturally affect the finished cost of the work. If you do decide on a change, ask for a new costing, and get this agreed in writing.

Finding space for an extra bathroom is top priority for many households. Ensure any hardcore work such as plumbing and wiring is completed before the decoration begins.

DRAWING UP A CONTRACT

Putting your agreement in writing can avoid potential problems once the work begins. If you draw up a contract with your builder or decorator make sure it includes:

☐ what work is to be done

☐ the hours the builders will work each day

☐ when the job will start and finish

☐ the total cost of the work and when the work will be paid for; this may be in instalments or as one payment at the end of the job

☐ what the complete job entails, for example whether you expect the contractors to clean and tidy the area and remove all rubbish before they leave

☐ available facilities for the builders; if they have to hire a portable WC, for example, they should tell you how much it will cost.

Building an extension to your home or simply reconfiguring the existing space by knocking down internal walls can give you the freedom to create a large, open-plan kitchen/dining room.

When to pay

While you should never pay for the whole job up front, be aware that payments in instalments is a reasonable request for a small building firm working on a large project. For small jobs, agree a small sum in advance to pay for any materials, then the pay the remainder when the job is satisfactorily completed.

MANAGING BIGGER PROJECTS

While it is wonderful to place your stamp on your home by redecorating, sometimes structural alterations are essential to make the best of your home. Knocking down walls or increasing space can help change the way you live at home for the better.

TYPES OF STRUCTURAL CHANGES

The conversion of a loft or the removal of a load-bearing wall can increase the available space or alter the current layout to make it more suitable for your lifestyle, but such work is also disruptive, and needs detailed planning and preparation.

Building work usually falls into four categories:

Remodelling existing rooms: this includes: knocking down internal walls, for example creating one large kitchen/diner out of two smaller rooms; putting up internal walls; installing an en-suite bathroom in a bedroom; or putting in a downstairs cloakroom. Remodelling is a good solution if you're happy with your available space, but you'd like to change the layout.

Permission granted

Large-scale building projects often require some form of official permission. Because the law varies from area to area it's important you follow up-to-date advice. Your local authority or, if you prefer, a recommended architect or other qualified professional such as a building surveyor, should be able to advise you on what is likely to be approved. Architects can also draw up plans, handle the submission to the relevant authorities, and recommend local building firms.

Converting unused space: this covers loft, basement and garage conversions, where existing unused space is turned into a new living area, such as an extra bedroom, home office or bathroom.

Extending your property: permanent single- or two-storey extensions are usually covered by strict planning guidelines, such as the size of the extension in relation to the existing size of your house. You will need to contact your local authority for information about property extension work in your area (see box).

Adding a conservatory: in general, conservatories have fewer strict planning guidelines than other extensions; again, talk to your local planning authority. You may find a conservatory provides you with the ideal extra space in your home without the additional hassle of seeking full-scale planning approval for the work.

Opening up unused attic space gives you the opportunity to increase the living area of your home.

BUDGETING

Setting the budget before you begin work enables you to keep control of the project. Architects and builders will give you quotes for their work, and you may also need to set aside part of the budget for materials, if you are sourcing these yourself. It's a good idea to keep back a small amount of the budget in case something goes wrong: 10 per cent of the total cost is a standard amount recommended.

Knocking several smaller rooms into one large space is a popular way to create a contemporary open-plan living area.

If you live in a terraced house, the builders and all their materials will have to enter and leave the house from the front door. Start projects towards the rear of the house.

Stress busters

Stress busting ideas for coping with building work include:

• Move out of your home during the work
• Draw up a contract
• Keep talking to your builders
• Be clear about your aims for the project.

PROJECT MANAGEMENT

Having builders in your house can be extremely stressful, even if everything is going to plan. A large building project needs a project manager, who's responsible for the day-to-day dealings with the building team, and who needs to be close to the site and able to visit it regularly. If you can't do this yourself, consider appointing an architect or building surveyor to do the job for you.

BEFORE WORK STARTS

Some jobs should logically take place before others (see page 183), but this order may be influenced by the complexity and scale of the work, the layout of your home and your lifestyle. Points to consider include:

Access points: terraced homes with only one door to the street may benefit from the work starting at the top and moving downwards, to avoid new surfaces on the lower floors being damaged by building work taking place above. Detached homes with several doors to the garden or street can be tackled in a different way; you may want to start at the furthest point from the builders' access, and work towards their entry point.

Where you will live: if the work to be done is extensive and disruptive, do you need to move out while it takes place? Alternatively, if you have space, you could arrange for one part of the house to be worked on at a time, so that you can move into one area when it is completed and work can start on another area. The builders and decorators will need to know if this is your plan, so they can adjust work schedules appropriately.

Small feet: pets, children and building sites don't mix. Ensure you can keep your pets and children away from any potential dangers.

GETTING READY FOR THE BUILDERS

Consider whether you're prepared to let the builders use your kitchen and bathroom. If not, tell them in advance so they can make other arrangements. Empty wardrobes and bookshelves, and move small items of furniture; the builders may help you with the larger items. Remember they'll also need clear access to the work area, so take down pictures on hallways and landings, for example, if they'll regularly be taking building materials through the house and up the stairs.

WORK IN PROGRESS

If you're planning on moving out from your home while the work takes place then it's important that you visit the site regularly, staying in touch with the team and keeping

Involving an architect to help you with your home renovation can result in some dramatic uses of the space.

abreast of the work that's taking place. If you're not happy with the work in progress, speak to the contractor in charge as soon as possible. Problems between contractors and clients often arise due to a lack of understanding between both sides. Ensure you are completely clear about what you are not happy with and that they understand what has gone wrong. If your builder attempts to guess what you would like, he is more likely to end up not pleasing you and the work will need to be redone.

Be clear on how you'd like them to treat your house while they're working there, from which door they should use to come into the house to protecting floors with boards and dust sheets.

Remember that there may be hitches plus unexpected complications such as bad weather conditions. Be prepared for these and factor in a little leeway in the time schedule.

When the job is finished make sure the contractor has completed all the tasks that were initially agreed, and has given you any necessary certificates to guarantee the work.

Keep your neighbours happy
Discuss your plans with your neighbours in advance, especially if the work affects them, for example if the builders will need to erect scaffolding on their land. When the work begins ensure your builders are considerate, cleaning up after themselves in any shared areas and keeping noise to a minimum.

BRIGHT IDEAS
DIY QUICK REFERENCE GUIDE

Decorating your home yourself is a wonderful way to save money, and a job well done will give you a real sense of achievement. If you're new to DIY, then start with the easy tasks. Painting, wallpapering and simple tiling can all be tackled by enthusiastic amateurs, as long as you follow the basic procedures outlined over these pages.

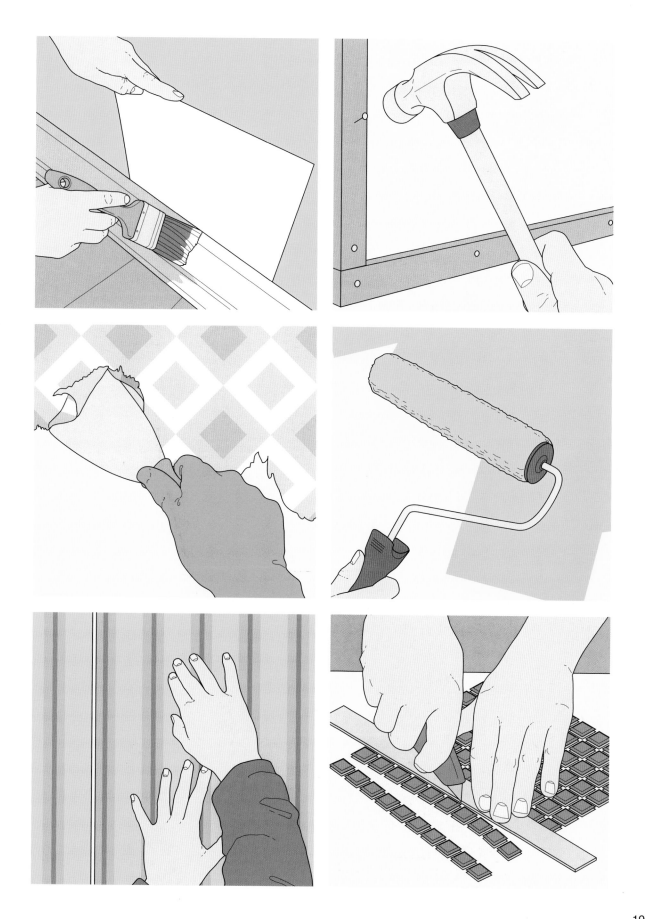

PAINTING

Painting is one of the quickest and easiest ways to bring colour and life to your rooms and most home-owners are willing to tackle it, but if you're a DIY novice there are some useful things to bear in mind.

PREPARATION

Preparing the surfaces is vitally important to ensure a professional-style finish to your job. Start in the following order:

☐ Assemble all your equipment, from ladders to paint and paintbrushes.

☐ Clear the area. Group furniture in the centre of the room, and cover it with dust sheets. Take down curtains and pictures, and cover the floors with fabric or plastic dust sheets.

☐ Clean the walls: dust them first, then wash them with a non-abrasive detergent such as sugar soap to remove any grease and grime.

☐ Remove picture pins or hooks, then fill holes and any cracks with a sandable filler. When it's dry, sand the area smooth so it's flush to the wall surface.

EQUIPMENT

☐ dust sheets

☐ enough paint for at least the first coat (see page 176 for how to calculate paint quantities)

☐ small paintbrushes: smaller ones for edges of walls and woodwork, plus larger ones for the main expanses, or a roller and tray (see box)

☐ ladder

☐ rags for mopping up splashes

☐ masking tape

☐ white spirit or turpentine to clean your brushes if you're using oil-based paint

☐ old clothes

Rollers or paintbrushes?

Brushes: in store you will find a wide selection of brushes, from disposable nylon-bristled brushes through to expensive versions made with animal hair. A mid-priced brush should be of good enough quality for domestic DIY.

Rollers: disposable rollers may be good for one-off jobs, but if you're planning on painting more than one room invest in a good-quality roller. Sleeves made from genuine sheepskin hold more paint than synthetic sleeves, but whichever you choose go for a sleeve with medium pile if you're applying emulsion.

A larger brush or roller will mean your job is done more quickly, as these carry more paint and so cover the walls more quickly, but very large rollers and brushes can be heavy. Amateur DIYers should consider starting with a 225 mm (9 in) roller or 100 mm (4 in) brush, while those with more experience can go for a 300 mm (12 in) roller or 150 mm (6 in) brush.

It's up to you whether you prefer to paint the main body of the walls with a roller or a paintbrush, but whichever you choose you will also need a small paintbrush for 'cutting in' along the edges of the walls and around light switches, and brushes for woodwork. Three widths should give you all the selection you need: 12, 25 and 50 mm (½, 1 and 2 in).

Tip
Always wash walls upwards: the water will disperse as it reaches the wet area below. If it runs on to a dry surface it may dry in dirty drip marks which will show through the new paint.

Painting the wall above a bed creates the illusion of a headboard and draws attention to the double bed. Soft lilac is an ideal shade for creating a calm bedroom.

The order of painting a room is:
1. ceiling **2.** walls **3.** window frame **4.** doors **5.** ceiling mouldings, picture rails **6.** skirtings **7.** radiators.

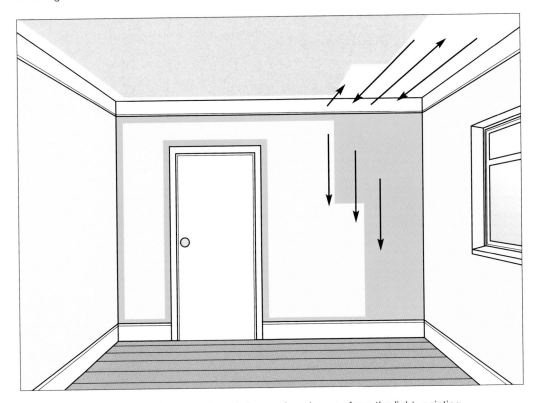

Paint ceilings in the corner closest to the window and work away from the light, painting in strips. For walls, start at a top corner and work towards a doorway, painting in strips.

PAINTING A ROOM
PAINTING CEILINGS AND WALLS

Low ceilings can be painted with a roller attached to an extension pole. For high ceilings, a scaffold board placed across two stepladders is a safer choice than a single ladder.

1. Dip the paintbrush in the can so that around a third to a half of the bristles are coated in paint. Dab any excess off gently on the inside edge of the can. If you're working with a roller, first pour a small amount of the paint into the well of the roller tray. Dip the roller sleeve in the well of the tray, then run the roller across the slope of the tray until the surface of the sleeve is evenly covered in paint.

2. To paint the ceiling, start in a corner near to the window, and work away from the light. Paint the edges first with a small brush, known as 'cutting in' (see below). Then use a larger brush or roller to paint the ceiling in bands around 60 cm (2 ft) wide, blending the edges together as you work.

3. For walls, start in a top corner near a window. Work from the top of the wall downwards, cutting in with a small brush first (see below) and then filling in the body of the walls with a large brush or roller. Again, work in strips about 60 cm (2 ft) wide, blending the edges together. When using a brush to cover the main expanse of wall, apply emulsion paint in parallel strokes, then finish with light strokes in all directions to feather the edges of the strokes and ensure an even, unlined finish.

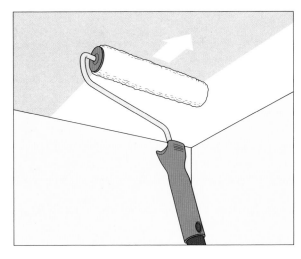

When using a roller, work in straight lines on the ceiling.

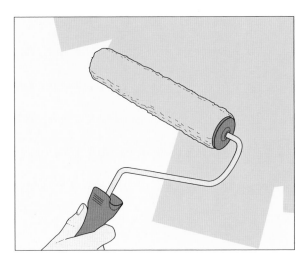

On walls, apply the paint in a criss-cross pattern, blending the edges of the paint and filling any gaps. Don't overload the roller with paint or it will splatter.

Cutting in

Using a narrow brush to paint the edges of walls and ceilings and around 'intrusions' such as light switches makes the painting job easier and neater. You will get a more professional finish if you cut in on small areas, paint the area with the roller or larger brush, then cut in the next area, progressing logically around the room. This way you will avoid an obvious banding effect that could occur around the edge of the walls.

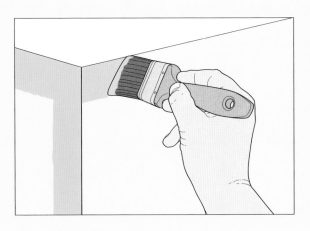

PAINTING WOODWORK

Paint picture rails and any wooden ceiling mouldings first, and skirting boards last. You may need to use a selection of small brushes (see page 194) depending on the detailing on your woodwork.

1. Remove any window catches or door handles.

2. You may want to use masking tape around the window edges to protect the glass. If you do, remove this when the paint is touch dry. Use a scalpel to carefully remove any dry paint on the glass.

3. When painting skirtings, hold a piece of card above the skirting board to protect the wall from any splashes of paint.

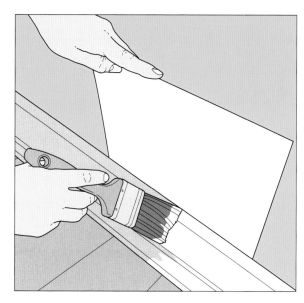

PAINTING RADIATORS

Paint radiators once the walls are completed. You can paint them with both water-based and oil-based paints, using a brush or a specially designed radiator roller. Don't apply the paint too thickly as this may make it run or wrinkle. Painting behind radiators is most easily done with a special, long-handled, mini roller.

CLEANING UP

Water-based paints: wash brushes and rollers in warm soapy water and rinse thoroughly.

Oil-based paints: place brushes in a solvent such as white spirit, loosening the paint from the bristles. For rollers, pour paint thinner into the roller tray, then roll the sleeve over it. Wash both rollers and brushes in warm soapy water, rinse and leave to dry.

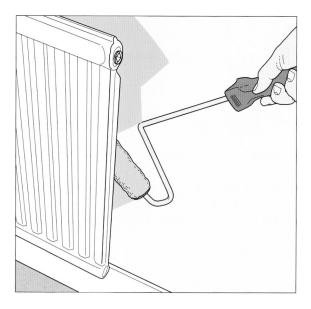

Painting insider info

• Don't overload the brush or roller as the paint will drip and the wall will be unevenly covered.
• Don't paint after dusk, if possible; poorly lit rooms can result in a patchy finish.
• Work in sections around the room, and stop at logical points, such as in a corner.
• Paint often looks patchy as it dries, but don't touch it up until the first coat is completely dry.
• It's likely you will need more than one coat to get the colour depth right.

Paint hallways, stairwells and landings in the same shade to create a feeling of unity between the two floors of the house.

WALLPAPERING

If you're new to wallpapering, try starting with a wallpaper that has a random pattern, as this won't require you to match up any patterns on the edges. This will make it much easier and quicker to hang.

PREPARATION

As with most DIY jobs, the more time you spend preparing the walls prior to papering them, the better the finished wall will look. You may need to:

☐ Strip old wallpaper using either warm water and a scraper, or a steam stripper and a scraper: a steam stripper makes the job easier if the old wallpaper is thick or has been painted.

☐ Wash the walls to remove traces of old adhesive.

☐ Fill any cracks and sand them so they are flush to the wall.

☐ Remove fittings such as wall lights, shelves, picture pins and roller blinds.

☐ Remove as much furniture as possible, or gather it together in the centre of the room, then cover it with dust sheets.

☐ When stripping old paper, cover the floor first with plastic, then with fabric dust sheets, to protect the flooring and prevent it becoming too slippery.

EQUIPMENT

☐ ladder, stepladder or two ladders and a scaffold board, depending on the area to be papered

☐ pasting table

☐ suitable adhesive, such as wallpaper paste

☐ large bucket and stirrer, or water trough for ready-pasted papers

☐ paste brus

☐ tape measure, pencil

☐ plumb line

☐ paper-hanging brush (for smoothing)

☐ sponge

☐ long-handled scissors, such as paperhanging shears

☐ seam roller

Tip
Stripping old wallpaper uses a lot of water. For safety, turn off the electricity at the mains before stripping paper around sockets and switches.

OPPOSITE Shimmering metallic wallpapers are ideal for bringing a touch of glitz and glamour to bedrooms.

Tip
Scoring the paper gently with the edge of your wallpaper scraper before you soak the walls lets the water permeate the paper and get to the adhesive behind, making it easier to remove the paper.

STRIPPING WALLPAPER

Soak the old paper in warm water to loosen the adhesive that's holding it in place on the walls.

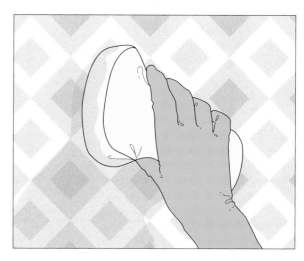

1. Saturate a large brush or sponge with warm water; if you wish, add some mild detergent to speed up the process. Move around the room, working from top to bottom.

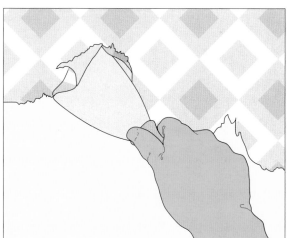

2. Remove the soaked paper by carefully scraping it off using a wallpaper scraper, making sure you don't gouge holes in the wall behind as you do so.

3. You may find it easier to hire a steam stripper, which speeds up the stripping process considerably. Hold the stripper up to the wallpaper so the steam can penetrate the paper. Then remove the paper with the scraper.

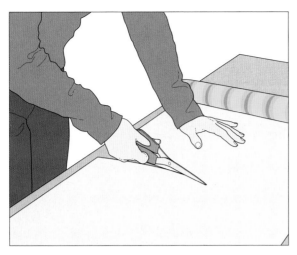

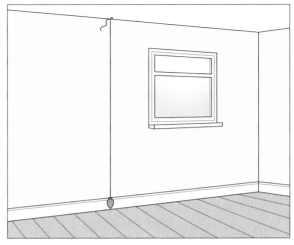

HANGING WALLPAPER

1. Measure the drop of the walls and add on an extra 10 cm (4 in) to allow for trimming the paper at the top and bottom once it's hung.

2. Unroll the paper, pattern side down, on the table. Measure and mark the drop length on the back of the paper, then cut with shears. Cut several lengths at a time so the next piece can soak while you hang the previous piece. Number the cut pieces on the reverse so you paste them on to the wall in the correct order.

3. It's important that your wallpaper is hung exactly vertically. Don't follow lines of window or door frames as these may well not be vertical, especially in older homes. To establish a vertical line at your starting point, hang a plumb line by a pin at the top of the wall. Draw in its vertical line on the wall with a soft pencil or piece of chalk. You will need to repeat this every time you start papering a new wall in the room.

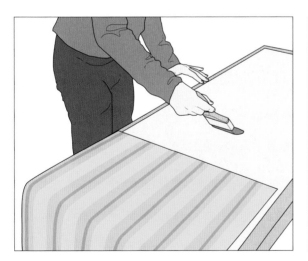

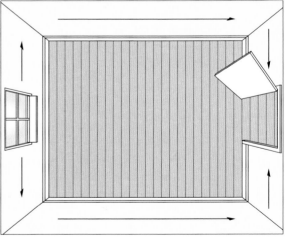

4. Lay your first length of cut paper pattern side down lengthways on the table. Using a generous amount of paste, paste the paper evenly along the middle, then outwards towards the paper edges. Ensure the paper is completely covered. Loosely fold the ends of the paper in towards the middle and allow it to soak for the recommended time: this can be up to ten minutes if the paper is very thick.

5. If your room has a focal point such as a fireplace in the centre of the main wall, start there. Hang the first piece so that your pattern falls in the centre of the chimney breast, then work outwards, papering in both directions towards the far wall or door. If there's no focal point, start papering to the right of the largest window. Work around the room until you reach the door, then go back to the first drop and work in the other direction.

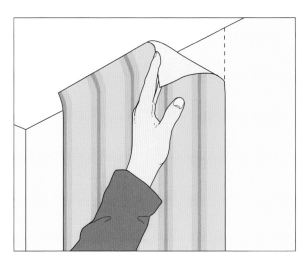

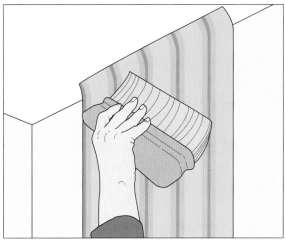

6. Unfold the top half of the pasted paper and position it on the wall so the edge is aligned with your vertical guideline, leaving a small overhang of about 5 cm (2 in) at the top so you can trim the paper.

7. Smooth the paper downwards, and then outwards, with a paper hanging brush. Open the bottom fold of the paper, and smooth the lower half of the length carefully into place.

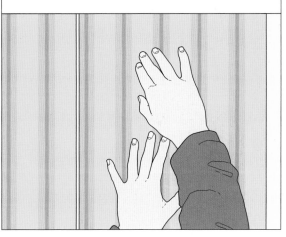

8. Where the paper joins the ceiling at the top and the skirting at the bottom, run the back of your shears along the paper. Peel back the paper and cut along the crease. Smooth the paper back in place and sponge off any excess paste immediately.

9. Hang the next length of pasted paper by sliding it into place so that it is positioned edge to edge with the first piece of paper with no overlap or gap. Brush the join to smooth the edges. You can also use a seam roller to press the edges (except on embossed paper).

Tip
To avoid pasting the table, align one edge of the paper with the table's edge. Paste this edge, then pull the paper so it aligns with the other table edge, and paste the second edge.

PAPERING AROUND AN INTERNAL CORNER

Wrapping a large piece of wallpaper around a corner looks messy. Instead, when you get to a corner, measure the distance from the edge of the last full piece of wallpaper to the corner itself. Add 1 cm (½ in) to this measurement. Cut the next piece of wallpaper to this width. Hang the paper so that the cut edge overlaps the corner.

The next length (you can use the offcut if it is wide enough) should cover this small overlap – remember to check it's vertical rather than being guided by the corner. Then continue papering around the room.

Wallpapering insider info

• Ready-pasted vinyl paper is the easiest type of wallpaper to hang. As its name suggests, there's no need to paste it, and the paper is tough and so less likely to tear while you're working with it.
• A simple design, such as a stripe, is an easy pattern to start with, as it's reasonably easy to join the edges of two drops together.
• Study the paper carefully before you start cutting and pasting to ensure you have the pattern the right way up. Once you've cut your lengths, write 'top' in pencil on the back of the paper at the top of each one.
• Clear up the trimmings as you work, so the floor does not get covered in lots of sticky pieces of pasted wallpaper.
• Wipe the pasting table regularly to remove splashes of wet paste before it dries and hardens.
• Once the paper has been hung and has dried, gently prick any remaining air bubbles with a pin, and smooth the paper flat.

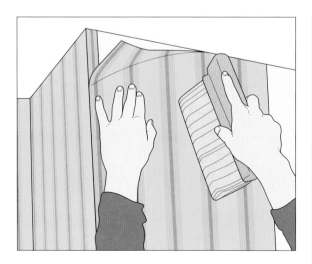

PAPERING AN EXTERNAL CORNER

The same principle applies, but allow a slightly larger overlap of around 2.5 cm (1 in). Paste the overlapping strip and smooth it around the corner. Position the offcut on the adjacent wall so that it overlaps the turned edge by about 1 cm (½ in).

Pattern repeats

If your wallpaper has no pattern repeat that needs matching, you can cut entire rolls into lengths all at once. When working with a wallpaper with a repeating design, you will need to allow more than the 10 cm (4 in) trim at top and bottom, to ensure you can match the repeat.

If you have chosen a complicated or large repeat, it is advisable to cut and hang the first length on the wall, and then match the next piece to it when it is in place. Double check the pattern match is correct – with dense or complex patterns it is surprisingly easy to mismatch or to paste a length upside down.

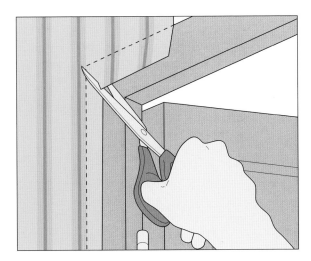

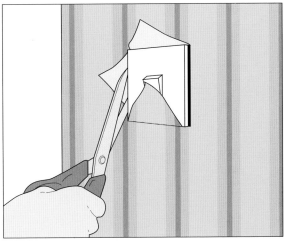

PAPERING AROUND A DOOR

When you reach the area of wall by the door frame, hang the paper in the usual way, with one edge next to the previous piece of paper. The other edge of the paper will overhang the door frame. Cut off most of the excess to within 2.5 cm (1 in) of the frame, and then make a diagonal cut in the excess paper, towards the corner of the door frame. Use the back of your shears to make a crease in the paper along the top and the side of the door frame. Peel the paper back to a smaller overlap (about 1 cm/½ in is plenty), then smooth the paper in place with the brush.

PAPERING AROUND A LIGHT SWITCH OR SOCKET

Swich off the mains electricity supply. Loosen the cover plate so you can tuck the paper behind it. Hang the length of paper then make a small diagonal cross in the paper. Trim back the paper leaving about 1 cm (½ in), and tuck this in behind the plate, smoothing it in place. Retighten the screws on the plate.

Tip

If you have a recessed window you may want to paper the internal wall area around the window frame, which is known as the reveal. Follow the numbered sequence in the diagram opposite, allowing for small overlaps where indicated by the dotted line. Windows that sit almost flush with the wall can be treated in the same way as when papering a door frame.

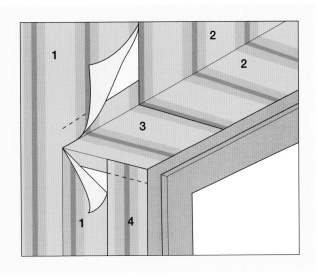

TILING

While tiles on walls and floors are usually reserved for wet areas such as kitchens and bathrooms, you can tile any flat surface as long as it is dry and clean. If you've never tiled before, start with a small area such as a splashback in a kitchen or behind a bathroom basin.

PREPARATION

As with any other form of wall treatment, careful preparation makes all the difference. Before applying new tiles the surface needs to be clean, dry and flat.

☐ Wear safety goggles and remove old tiles with a club hammer and bolster chisel.

☐ Depending on the condition of the plaster, fill small holes and cracks or replaster.

☐ Seal bare plaster and plasterboard with either a coat of PVA sealer or a coat of emulsion.

☐ Wash painted walls. If you're concerned that the paint is too slick, key the surface with coarse sandpaper: this will help the adhesive to grip to painted walls.

☐ Wallpapered walls will need to be stripped and made good in preparation for tiling.

EQUIPMENT

To cut tiles:

☐ felt-tip pen

☐ tile cutter

☐ tile nibbler

☐ tile saw

☐ tile file or coarse sandpaper

☐ tile scorer

To fix tiles:

☐ spirit level

☐ tape measure

☐ pencil

☐ timber battens, 1.2 m long by 5 x 2.5 cm (4 ft long by 2 x 1 in)

☐ hammer

☐ long masonry nails

☐ adhesive

☐ spreader (this usually comes inside the tub of adhesive)

☐ sponge

☐ dry cloth

☐ grout

☐ tile spacers

Tip

Hand-made tiles bought from the same batch can still have variations in colour. Unpack all the packs of tiles and shuffle them so the colour or pattern differences are spread evenly across the tiled area.

APPLYING TILES TO WALLS

It's imperative that you fix wall tiles so they are level both horizontally and vertically, but because the floor or skirtings are unlikely to be level you can't use these as your guideline. Instead, you need to fix wooden battens as a temporary straight edge for the first row of tiles.

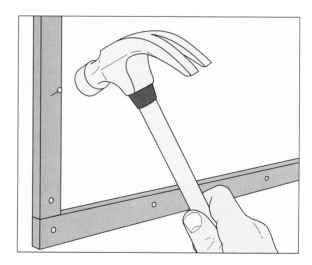

1. Tiles are hung from the bottom of the wall upwards. To establish a horizontal base for your first row, measure one tile depth upwards from the base of your floor (or worktop or skirting). Fix a temporary batten to the wall with its upper edge at this height. Check it is horizontal with a spirit level and hold it in place with masonry nails (leave the nails protruding so they are easy to remove later). Fit a vertical batten in the same way, or use a plumb line and draw in the vertical line.

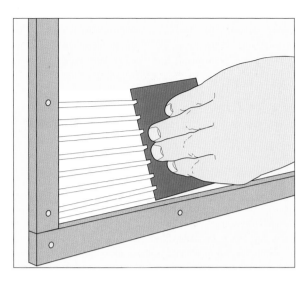

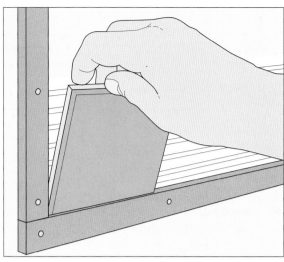

2. Starting in the corner where your battens meet, apply tile adhesive to the wall with the notched spreader, covering about 1 sq m or 1 sq yd at a time.

3. Place the first tile on the wall where the battens meet, and press it firmly into place.

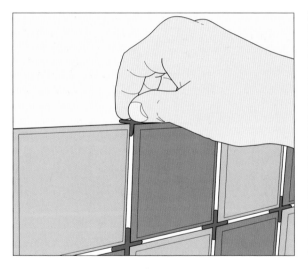

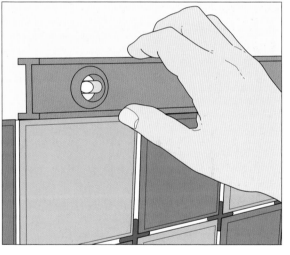

4. Continue tiling, inserting spacers between the top corners, and positioning the next tile so that it sits close to the spacer. Tile the area with whole tiles, leaving spaces for any that need to be cut to size: you will return and do these later.

5. Use the spirit level regularly to check that the tiles are aligned both vertically and horizontally.

6. Remove the battens and tile the lowermost row, together with any tiles which needed to be cut (see page 209). For these last stages you may find it easier to apply the adhesive to the back of the tile rather than to the wall.

Tip

Tiles can be fixed on top of a layer of existing tiles, as long as the existing tiles are firmly attached. Rub down the old tiles with coarse silicon-carbide paper to key the surface ready for tiling.

7. When the adhesive is dry remove the spacers. Use a damp sponge to apply the grout, pressing it firmly into the gaps between the tiles.

8. Use a rounded stick to press the grout in place and to give the tiles a professional finish. Before the grout dries, wipe the tiles over with a damp cloth to remove any smears of grout on their surface.

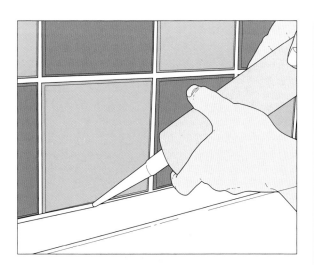

9. To finish, seal the gap between the tiled area and the adjacent surface with silicone rubber sealant. Apply the sealer in one continuous line, drawing the nozzle along the bottom edge of the tiles.

Tiling insider info

• Don't spread too much adhesive on the walls at once, as it dries quickly. Tiles stuck to partially dry adhesive are unlikely to bond well and may fall off.

• If you need to drill into tiles, mark a cross on the tile with masking tape, then drill through this: the tape stops the drill bit from slipping.

• Floor tiles are heavier than wall tiles, which are too thin to be walked on. While you can tile a wall in floor tiles, it's better to pick the right tile for the surface you are decorating.

Making a tiling gauge

A tiling gauge is easy to make and helps you work out how and where to place the tiles.

Lay a row of tiles on the floor along the edge of one of the battens, just as you plan to arrange them on the surface you're tiling. Insert spacers between each tile, then mark on the batten the widths of the tiles and the grouting space between. You can then hold this up to the wall and see at a glance how many tiles will fit into that space, and where to place any cut tiles.

CUTTING A STRAIGHT EDGE

Hold the tile to the wall and measure it against the gap so you can see how much tile you will need to cut off. Mark the cutting line on the tile with a pencil. Place the tile on a flat surface, decorative side up, and score a line through the glaze using a tile scorer. Place a matchstick under each end of the tile in line with the score mark, and press down on either side so it cleanly snaps in two.

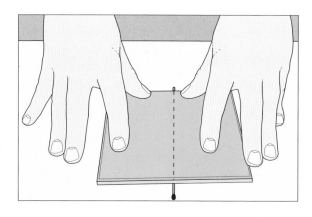

CUTTING A CURVED OR ANGULAR SHAPE

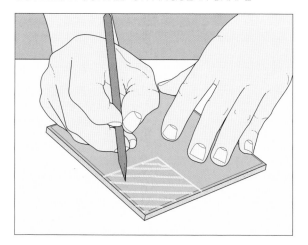

1. Mark the shape to be cut on the tile, and then score along the cut line as before with tile scorers. Make criss-cross scores over the surplus piece.

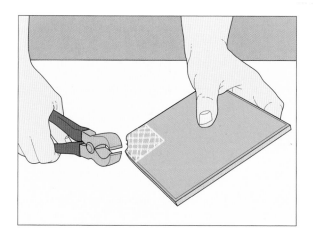

2. Nibble away the excess with tile nibblers, or use a tile saw.

FIXING MOSAIC TILES

1. Mosaic tiles usually come in sheet form, stuck on a mesh backing, which is cut to size. They are put up in the same way as standard ceramic tiles.

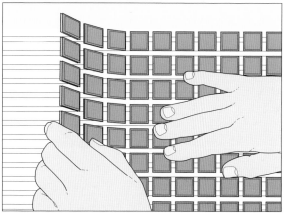

2. Spread adhesive on the wall. Making sure the arrows on the backs of the sheets face in the same direction, press each sheet firmly into place, aligning them carefully. Small areas will need to be cut to size. Grout as before.

FAST FIXES AND FINISHING TOUCHES

THE FINAL DETAILS

Once the decorators have departed, your hard work is finished and it's time to have some fun. Finishing touches are essential, and it's these accessories and details that add an extra injection of vitality and personality to a room.

ADDING THAT FINISHING TOUCH

If you are unsure about what's missing from your completed room, ask the advice of friends and family. They may point out aspects which you had overlooked, such as a dark corner which could be easily brightened with an extra floor lamp, or an empty wall that's ideal for your framed set of wedding photographs.

You will also discover as you use the room what finishing touches you would like to add. Look at all the walls and floors – could you brighten up the room with a new rug, or add a series of photos or prints to a bare wall? Mirrors will always help a small room appear larger, but could you hang a picture on the opposite wall which reflects back into the mirror? Consider other surfaces, too, such as coffee and side tables, windowsills, mantelpieces and shelves. If they are covered in items you don't like and never look at, get rid of them and replace them with things that you do love. Now is the chance to build up a collection of pieces that mean something to you, or to display your existing much-loved possessions with pride.

One of the best ways to bring life and vibrancy into any room is to add flowers and plants. Take a quick glance at the interiors of homes featured in magazines and you will see the rooms are often filled with flowers. Think along seasonal lines and treat yourself to a vase of brightly coloured blooms in the summertime, or gather rich foliage and berries during the winter. Plant up bulbs or rows of small bedding plants in pretty pots and planters to brighten up windowsills or stand in rows on a mantelpiece or table.

CLEARING UP CLUTTER

Keeping your rooms clean and clutter-free goes a long way towards making your home a pleasant place to live in. If you follow the maxim of William Morris, the Victorian designer and writer, you will be in good company. His golden rule for interior design was: 'Have nothing in your houses that you do not know to be useful or believe to be beautiful'. When you're thinking about what to get rid of, this is as useful a piece of advice today as it was in the nineteenth century.

Remove stacks of old magazines from coffee and bedside tables; blitz piles of filing; clean windows in preparation for new blinds or curtains; store unattractive paperwork in pretty filing boxes; chuck out metal clothes hangers and instead treat your clothes to chunky wooden hangers which not only look more attractive but also prolong the life of the clothes. Simple actions such as these take little time to do and all contribute to making every room more attractive and relaxing to use.

Edible aromatics

Scented herbs are both attractive and useful in the kitchen and make deliciously aromatic table decorations for a summertime lunch party.

A table placed in front of a sunny window is the ideal spot to display vases and glassware. Create a simple seaside-inspired display with a jam jar filled with shells and a casually assembled bunch of delicate summery flowers.

LEFT Start a collection of ornaments which look wonderful together and which suit your décor, such as an arrangement of unusually shaped ceramic vases and carafes.

RIGHT Create individual arrangements at each table setting by tying luxury chocolates into a pretty napkin and knotting with a length of glamorous ribbon.

THE ART OF DISPLAY

Display is all about bringing colour, pattern and personality to your home, livening up the rooms as you do so. The most successful displays of art and ornaments are where items are grouped together in an eye-catching, thought-provoking manner.

COLLECTIONS

It can be hard to know where to begin in a bare, newly decorated room, so a good starting point might be to think of what interests you and begin collecting pictures and ornaments based on a theme. This could involve art of all types, ranging from antique prints to family photographs, and from precious silver to pretty but inexpensive ceramics, and found objects.

As well as choosing a subject matter for your collection think about the style of images or ornaments which appeal to you. If you're a traditionalist you may prefer to collect antique prints, while those who love contemporary design may be drawn to modern media such as photographic images and abstract art. A love of pictures of people, for example, could open up a world of opportunities for collecting, from simple colour snaps of your family to traditional painted portraits or contemporary photographic images.

The search for the pictures and decorative objects is part of the fun, and you can build your collection up over many years. Buy pieces that you love rather than those you believe will be an investment. If they accrue in value then that's a bonus, but it's more important to enjoy looking at the pieces on display in your home.

Building up a collection of items that appeal to you personally ensures you will create a unique collection that's not only interesting to look at but which also reveals your interests and individual style. As the collection builds you will be able to rearrange the display, altering it as the seasons change and your lifestyle evolves, and so don't be afraid to get rid of pieces you no longer like.

PLACEMENT

The location of your display plays a large part in its success. You can either accumulate objects or paintings for a particular area or, if you have a collection already, think about the best place to site it from both a practical and visual perspective. A series of paintings of nudes can look stylish in a bathroom but might look out of place in a hallway, while delicate Chinese porcelain may look wonderful on a dining room dresser but needs to be kept out of the reach of small children.

Places in your home might reveal themselves to be the perfect location for a display: the wall above a fireplace, for example, is a natural focal point and is the ideal place to hang a large painting. Tiny nooks and crannies such as narrow shelves above doorways lend themselves to displaying quirky pieces of sculpture or vintage china.

LEFT This creamy white orchid brings a touch of oriental appeal to a corner of this sitting room. Following the maxim 'less is more' can result in a subtle and sophisticated display.

OPPOSITE This single wooden shelf behind a sofa is the ideal height to display pictures and ornaments in a living room. The mix of paintings, books, vases and bottles has been chosen in shades that coordinate with the room's décor, forming a display that's easily altered when it's time for a change.

PICTURES, PHOTOGRAPHS AND PAINTINGS

If you're buying a print, photograph or painting, you may need to get it framed. As a general rule, a picture frame should complement the picture or photograph, not distract attention from it. Large pictures often look best with a thin frame, while a small picture can be made to look more dramatic with an oversized mount and decorative frame. For a group of pictures that will be hung on the wall together, you can opt either to mix and match the frames for an eclectic look or give the group a cohesive look by choosing the same style of frame for each image.

Tip

Before you hang a group of pictures on the wall, first lie the paintings on the floor and work out the arrangement. This way you can play around with the arrangement before tapping the picture hooks into the wall. Horizontally arranged pictures give rooms the illusion of width, while hanging pictures vertically gives them the appearance of height.

Decide whether a picture will look best hung by itself or in a group together with similar pictures. Small pictures often look best hung in a group, while bright and busy pictures may need more space between them. Try a vertical line of three small prints, or a series of several grouped together to form a rectangular collection of images. When hanging pictures in a group, position them so they hang close to each other on the wall. This ensures the arrangement is seen as a whole, rather than as lots of smaller images. Pictures should be hung at eye level or below so you can see them properly, especially if the pictures are small. If you're planning on covering a whole wall in pictures, find the

Popular subjects for pictures

Gardens: a broad range of subjects and styles, from traditional botanical prints to contemporary horticultural images or romantic watercolours.

Celebrities: children love to paper their bedrooms with images of their favourite stars. Posters are ideal, as they are inexpensive and easy to replace.

Architecture: cityscapes in graphic black and white, architectural drawings or details, the evolution of your own house at different stages are all possible themes.

Portraits: your family, both present-day and going back through the generations, could be a rich and rewarding source of images.

Landscapes: whether painted, drawn or photographs, landscapes and seascapes are perennially popular images for our walls. These pictures can make great focal points.

Animals: from cheerful prints for children to quirky photographs, animals are always appealing.

Fashion and textiles: images, or displays, of vintage clothes and hats, or photographs of iconic fashion moments: all are perfect for bedrooms or dressing rooms.

LEFT Pictures don't have to be mounted and framed. Here three maps, printed on to canvas and left unframed, are hung in a row to bring some subtle colour and a sense of history into this home office.

KEY STYLE FEATURES

Hanging several pictures together in a group on one wall is a great way to give a room a focal point.

A visual link is provided by each picture's natural subject matter.

Several beautiful objects placed on the streamlined console table ensure that the entire wall becomes an attractive display area.

The symmetrical arrangement of a large picture framed on either side by two smaller ones balances the display.

LEFT Choosing pictures or ornaments with a common theme gives your display an obvious visual link. Placing the pictures on a shelf, rather than hanging them on the wall above, lends an informal air to the overall display.

stairs. Passageways such as hallways and landings are a good location for a series of similarly shaped pictures.

Artwork doesn't have to be hung directly on wall. An open shelf provides an alternative and effective way to display a collection of pictures. It also gives you the opportunity to include other ornaments such as vases and china that can't be part of a wall-mounted arrangement. Placing the pictures directly on the shelf gives the display area an informal look and it can be easily altered and adapted.

When fitting a shelf, think about its height: you want to be able to see the display when you are in the room. In living rooms a low shelf fixed behind a sofa is an ideal place for a mix of pictures and ornaments, while in kitchens, where you're more likely to be standing, a shelf at just above radiator height is a good spot for a collection of family snaps and children's artwork.

centre of the wall and work outwards in both directions from there. Use proper picture hooks (you may need two when hanging larger pictures). Screws for heavy mirrors and paintings may need to be fixed into the wall with wall plugs.

Staircases are ideal for displaying a series of pictures; the open expanse of wall space and the movement of people from one floor to the next means the pictures will be constantly admired. Hang them so they step upwards, with each picture slightly higher than the last, creating a sense of movement up the

Insider info

Don't hang pictures or photographs above radiators or in direct sunlight as this will cause them to age. Humidity can also age pictures, so be careful about placing treasured artwork or photographs in steamy bathrooms.

RIGHT Use mirrors as part of your display, and simultaneously increase the sense of light and airiness in your rooms.

DISPLAYING ORNAMENTS AND FOUND OBJECTS

Pretty much anything that is collectable can go on display. Salvage yards, flea markets, bric-a-brac stalls and modern design emporia are all hunting grounds for objects from antique porcelain to contemporary glassware, or vintage clothing and toys to retro and cutting-edge design classics.

Everyday items can be displayed in inventive ways just as successfully as artistic or collected treasures. Books are a constant favourite; the expression 'books do furnish a room' holds good, whether it applies to shelves filled with rows of antique hardbacks or second-hand paperbacks with colourful spines, a library

When setting up a display, think of how the various elements will work together as a whole. Several different flower arrangements are grouped on this side table alongside an eclectic mix of books, artwork and china, but together they create an attractive, harmonious display.

of children's classics or glossy coffee table books that get their nickname from where they're displayed. Think about the effect of CDs and DVDs in contemporary shelving that makes a feature of the repetitive lines of the discs. Bring nature indoors: spring bulbs or found objects such as shells and fir cones all add their own textures, scents and colours to your room scheme.

KEY STYLE FEATURES

Cube shelving units are ideal for displaying a collection of objects in a living room.

The books, china and ornaments on display have been chosen in a mix of white, red and black, to reflect the room's colour scheme.

The edge of each cube provides a frame for the item or items it contains, but also links it, through harmonious repetition, to the other articles on display.

The adjacent wall is the perfect spot for a pair of large black and white photographic images of ferns.

RIGHT A display can be as simple as these earthy-toned vessels grouped together on a wicker tray, and the smoothness of the glass contrasts pleasingly with the textural qualities of the mother-of-pearl and the wickerwork.

When you are putting together items for display, think about colour, pattern and texture, just as you did when you were decorating. Providing visual links between the objects helps unify the collection, while adding some contrast brings the display to life. Placing decorative objects among more mundane ones turns a practical storage area into an eye-catching focal point. You can also use the display to bring toning or contrasting textures and colour to a room: imagine a selection of colourful vases that contrast with the wall colour, or a tactile mix of natural objects arranged together on a side table. In public spaces such as hallways, the occasional quirky find will catch your visitors' eyes, while in private rooms a selection of objects that bring back memories can create a space for recollection and thought.

Tips for displaying

• Site displays on surfaces that are visible, so they can be enjoyed by everyone in the room.
• Make sure the displays aren't in the way. The surfaces of coffee tables, for example, are functional places for cups, magazines and remote controls, so ensure any displays leave room for the practicalities of life.
• Think about how you use the room: don't place fragile ornaments where they can be broken.
• Consider a potential spot for a picture or ornament from where you most often sit or stand: this can influence the height and the location of the display area.
• Lighting can be used very effectively to highlight your displays, simultaneously turning them into a focal point and bringing extra atmosphere to the room at night.

LEFT Details can influence the mood of a room. Here, the neutral tones and organic, natural shapes of a few understated items brought together subliminally enhance the sense of calmness in the room.

ACCESSORIES

Your choice of toiletries and towels, cushions and throws, tablecloths and bedlinen add life and interest to a room and turn a house into a home. Accessories can be inexpensive or priceless, but whichever you choose make sure that they suit the room.

SHOPPING AROUND

Whatever your budget, shopping for accessories should be considered a work in progress, with items bought as and when you see them, or as your likes evolve or your lifestyle changes.

Search for accessories wherever you can: antiques markets are filled with quirky extras you won't find elsewhere; modern interiors shops are good for both inexpensive buys and up-to-the-minute designer pieces; while online shopping is a great way to source items from shops that you aren't physically able to visit. For one-off pieces such as antiques, vintage or secondhand buys, it usually pays to buy when you see them as the items may not be available when you return.

To prevent mistakes, especially with articles that are hard to return to the seller, such as boot-fair buys or those bought far from home, have a clear picture in your head of what exactly you think the room needs. Our memory of colour can be unreliable, so take swatches of your fabrics, paints or wallpapers with you when shopping so you can be certain of a colour match to what's already in the room: this is particularly helpful when buying soft furnishing accessories such as cushions, throws, rugs and bedlinen.

If you are on the look-out for a painting or picture for a particular wall, take measurements and keep these with you so you can work out whether a picture you like will fit the available space. Be aware of dimensions, both of your room and of the item you are buying, especially if you are buying online, and keep a measuring tape alongside your fabric swatches when shopping. You might find it helpful to photograph newly redecorated rooms: you can either take the prints or the camera with you when shopping, so a quick glance will refresh your memory of exactly how your room now looks.

Bear in mind how you wanted the room to look when you began to decorate. You might need to search out those magazine or book images which initially inspired you, in order to source accessories that capture the style.

A tight budget can encourage inventiveness. Consider how you can recycle your existing accessories to fit the newly decorated room. Changing picture frames and lightshades gives prints and lamps a completely new look, while confident seamstresses may be able to turn discarded curtains into cushion covers, or large bedspreads into smaller curtains. Think about swapping items from room to room, or even from house to house if you have friends with items they'd like to give to a new and welcoming home.

Adding accessories is one of the great pleasures of interior decorating, so be inspired to update your look with the clever fast fixes pictured on the following pages.

Well-chosen decorative details, enhanced by the large mirror, help turn this unused part of the bedroom into a fully functioning dressing table area. Make-up and toiletries are kept close to hand in the textured sisal baskets, while a silk cushion softens the practical stool.

LEFT Here a mix of visually interesting accessories, from china to prints, forms a striking monochrome display that instantly catches the eye.

RIGHT Choose accessories that suit the room's decorative scheme. These floral cushions add just the right amount of colour and pattern to lift this sitting room's delicately muted colour scheme.

DINING ROOMS AND KITCHENS

1   In open-plan shelf units, choose textured baskets to hide dull accessories from view, but let pretty china and vases be on display for all to see.

2   Add some comfort and prettiness to bench-style seating by placing a luxuriously covered cushion at each place setting.

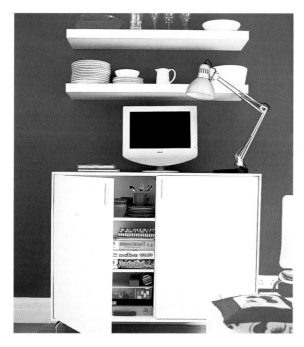

3   Display your best china on open shelves, saving cupboard space for storing children's utensils, games and toys.

4   Open wicker baskets are ideal for keeping all you need for setting the table close to hand, yet hidden from view when not in use.

5 A dramatic pendant lightshade draws attention to the dining area and ensures the table is the room's focal point whatever the time of day.

6 Colourful bunting brings a fun party atmosphere to a dining room. Peg cards to the bunting for a personal touch.

7 A series of photographs, such as this set of informal wedding shots, is a great way to bring a sense of welcome and conviviality to a dining room wall.

8 Suspend kitchen utensils and pans from wall-mounted hooks or racks hanging from the ceiling. A blackboard makes an attractive shopping list.

HALLWAYS

1 A set of hooks and a small table are essential items for keeping everyday hallway bits and pieces under control.

2 Hang one large mirror or a series of several small mirrors on the wall by the front door to bring light into a narrow or dark hallway.

3 Two sets of contemporary coat hooks keep this open-plan hallway floor clear of dropped bags and coats, leaving the space clutter-free.

4 Choose a dramatic lightshade; your hall is the first impression visitors get of your home, so be sure to wow guests with an eye-catching light fitting.

LIVING ROOMS

1 A collection of beautiful vases and bowls, each chosen for its sculptural shape, creates a serene display area.

2 A collection of different coloured and textured decorative balls brings colour, pattern, texture and visual interest to a coffee table.

3 Intersperse a display of books with photo frames. Books don't have to stand upright: laying some on their sides breaks up the rows.

4 Woollen blankets in neutral colours and hand-made cushions in the corner of the sofa create a cosy spot that's hard to resist when it's time to relax.

LIVING ROOMS

5 Display found objects and ornaments on the lower shelf of a coffee table, leaving the surface free for cups and glasses.

6 Make the most of the daylight which streams through your windows and use the sill to display a collection of brightly coloured glass.

7 Use translucent glass tiles as coasters, choosing them in a selection of jewel-bright shades to bring a splash of colour to your side tables.

8 During the summer exchange heavy drapes for floaty voiles, pulled back with a simple ribbon tie-back, to let the sunshine flood into the room.

9   Floor cushions make ideal extra seating. On winter nights place them so that guests can feel the welcoming warmth from the hearth.

10   Pick accessories in colours that coordinate with your décor; a mix of vases in berry red, deep brown and cream makes for a winning display.

11   Citrus shades add springtime zest to rooms. These fruits and flowers and lime-green runner create a combination that freshens up the entire room.

12   There's no need for formal magazine racks. A squishy sisal basket, placed close to the sofa's edge, keeps essential reading material close by.

LIVING ROOMS

13 Collect china by style, pattern or colour, such as this blue and white selection, and arrange it in groups for maximum impact.

14 Create contrast with different textures. Place smooth fabrics alongside ones with heavy detailing or a rough weave, such as wool, silk and satin.

15 Placing faux animal-hide cushions on a leather chair creates a mix of textures that's tactile and appealing.

16 Hang a group of similarly themed pictures in a vertical row to make a feature of an alcove area or to give your room the impression of height.

BEDROOMS

1 Dress up plain curtains by choosing a decorative tie-back to hold the curtains away from the window during the daytime.

2 Add sparkle to delicate sheer drapes with colourful glass beads, threaded on to tiny ribbons and hung from the bed frame or curtain pole.

3 Create a relaxing mood by hanging a delicate chandelier over a pendant light, so softening the harsh light that's often emitted by a single bulb.

4 Hang vintage mirrors together in groups on your bedroom wall for a unique display which also helps the room seem larger and brighter.

BEDROOMS

5 Pretty glass bottles and dishes for toiletries and make-up add glamour to a dressing table. Position them in front of a window so the glass sparkles.

6 Storage doesn't have to be dull. Choose attractive boxes that will fit beneath your bed to keep belongings out of the way, yet accessible.

7 Group ornaments and lighting together to create an illuminated display area that's attractive to look at both day and night.

8 Add some shimmer to your bedroom with a selection of luxurious quilts, cushions and bedlinen in glistening silks and satins.

9 Use surface space in bedrooms to display a mix of neutral-toned yet textured ornaments, to bring a sense of calm order to the room's scheme.

10 Give light fittings a new look by changing the shades; a delicate shade such as this will fill a bedroom with a subtle glow.

11 Start a display of ornaments and pictures which bring back happy memories, such as photos and mementoes of holidays.

12 A bedside storage basket is a good place to keep extra blankets and any other night-time essentials you may have.

HOME OFFICES

1   Choose box files that are covered in pretty fabrics to create a filing solution that looks too good to be hidden away.

2   Hanging two noticeboards near your work area – one for work, one for personal administration – means you can see at a glance what needs to be done.

3   File disks and samples in colourful card boxes to keep them together in one spot. If space allows, store them in out-of-the-way wall-mounted cube shelves.

4   Hang a simple noticeboard on the inside of a filing cupboard door to keep essential notes and memos easily visible.

BATHROOMS

1 Update your bathroom with wooden accessories that are smooth, streamlined and modern to bring a natural touch to the room.

2 A single pink rose – choose a scented variety if possible – and luxurious toiletries placed by the basin add a welcoming touch to cloakrooms.

3 For a touch of luxury, decant shampoo and foam bath into old-fashioned ceramic bottles, and display soap in sparkling glass dishes.

4 A simple wooden towel rail and unbleached cotton hammam towels create a spa-like ambience in the bathroom.

BRIGHT IDEAS
FAST FIXES

Use flowers, plants, candles and decorative details to bring a temporary change to the way your home looks. A table setting is the ideal way to make your dining area look delightfully seasonal, while candles can be used in every room in the home. Because the decorative setting is not designed to be permanent, you can afford to go for a look that's a little more lavish or ornate than your usual style.

TABLE SETTINGS

When it comes to setting the table, whether it's a springtime breakfast for two, a big family party or an evening meal with friends, a little attention to detail turns your table into a feast for the eyes.

CREATE A FESTIVE Christmas table by mixing red, white and natural wood accessories that are inspired by traditional Scandinavian design.

Dress the surrounding room with seasonal berries and foliage to complete the look.

Arrange a centrepiece of lanterns and berries to bring a warm glow to the table.

Swap a traditional full-size tablecloth for more informal table runners.

ADD A LITTLE ORIENTAL charm to your lunch time table setting with accessories chosen in delicate pink tones.

Place an orchid in the centre of the table.

With contemporary china and glassware chosen in muted tones of shell pink and jade green, and dipping bowls and chopsticks at each place setting, the oriental theme is complete.

Instead of a tablecloth, lay a length of iridescent wallpaper along the length of the table as a runner.

A SUMMERY MIX of creams, pinks and white makes this table perfect for a celebration party.

Suspend simple lanterns from the ceiling or, if outdoors, from nearby trees or the roof of a gazebo.

Arrange bunches of sweet-scented roses in pots along the table.

Scatter individual petals among the place settings.

KEY STYLE FEATURES

Jewel shades and plenty of sparkle create a party-time table setting.

Candles – illuminate the surrounding surfaces with a subtle arrangement of glass candlesticks.

For an inviting winter dinner table, set each place with glassware and plates in jewel bright shades of amethyst and fuchsia.

Suspend colourful baubles from the ceiling on long lengths of coloured ribbon for a dramatic centrepiece.

Scatter foil-wrapped chocolates for extra sparkle.

LEFT A glass bowl filled with frosted white and silver decorations makes an elegant centrepiece for a winter table setting.

BELOW Black and white is a sophisticated choice for an evening table setting. Choose a black tablecloth, and top with monochrome patterned tableware. Scatter silver-coated sugar almonds among the place settings for a touch of glitz.

ABOVE Turn party drinks into works of art by placing an exotic bloom in each glass, and scatter a handful of golden decorative baubles at the base.

KEY STYLE FEATURES

Decorate a table with brilliant tropical shades for a summer lunch with friends.

Tie colourful ribbons and paper flowers to each chair to add to the party atmosphere.

A simple fabric runner is less formal than a tablecloth.

Serving dishes in citrus shades add some zing to the setting.

Suspend brightly coloure paper lanterns above the

LEFT For a birthday breakfast on a sunny morning, set a bowl on top of a matching plate. Place a flower and napkin on top, and tie the setting in a long strip of gauzy ribbon.

BELOW Natural materials in neutral tones provide a pared-down look for an autumnal table. Choose elements such as dark wooden table mats and smooth wood-handled cutlery. Complete each place setting with a single fir cone for a seasonal touch.

ABOVE Choose pure linen and cream china for a simple, sophisticated place setting. Instead of a central floral arrangement, place a single rose in a glass by each place setting. Alongside handwritten place cards add a tiny sprig of foliage – a scented herb such as lavender or rosemary is ideal.

FLOWERS AND PLANTS

Flowers and plants bring nature indoors to remind us of the ever-changing seasons outside our windows and adding life, bright colours, patterns and wonderful scents to every room in the house.

FEW CAN RESIST an arrangement of roses, the most classic of flowers, with their beautiful blooms and gorgeous scent.

For added impact, group the arrangement with other taller glass vases.

Traditional large-headed roses in a dusky pink shade have everlasting appeal

A curvaceous dusky pink glass vase is perfect for displaying the simple arrangement of roses.

Create a unified display by adding toning scented candles, fallen petals and extras such as pretty books.

DRAMATIC FLOWERS such as orchids or amaryllis need very little arranging to make a stunning focal point.

Wire together just two or three amaryllis stems in a tall vase to create an almost instant arrangement.

Place the arrangement in front of a mirror to double the impact.

Add some trailing foliage to make a real eye-catcher of a display.

FOR A WINTER arrangement that's a little bit different, try these simple yet unusual greenery- and berry-filled paper cones.

Make the cones with circles of stiff paper.

Add a simple arrangement of berries and evergreen foliage such as ivy.

Suspend the cones on wire from the mantelpiece, or place them on the table as individual arrangements at each place setting.

FLOWERS AND PLANTS

Choose a stemmed clear-glass vase or dish and float in it a few flower heads, such as roses, for a look that's perfect for a mantelpiece in a feminine bedroom.

Posies of creamy white blooms look fresh and dainty. Group several together in a mix of cups and glasses for an informal floral display.

Choose quirky containers to create a joyful display. These pelargoniums look both appealing and cheerful in their teapot and watering can.

For triple impact, arrange ceramic pots of bulbs, such as these white hyacinths, in a row of three for a simple but compelling arrangement.

Place single stems of wild flowers and foliage in simple clear-glass bottles for a windowsill display that's pared down, pretty and calm.

A Moroccan tea glass makes a perfect delicate vase for scented blooms; place it on a bedside table as a thoughtful touch in a guest bedroom.

These glowing orange gerberas in their fuchsia-pink Chinese-lantern vase create a vibrant mix that's impossible to ignore.

A bunch of full-blown blooms casually arranged in an enamelware jug adds a cheerful touch to a summertime table setting.

CANDLES AND DECORATIONS

Use candles, decorative accessories and natural found objects imaginatively to add finishing touches that will bring style and glamour to your home throughout the year.

A FIREPLACE makes a dramatic centrepiece for a decorative display.

Candles along the mantelpiece echo the flames from the fire.

Foliage sprayed silver sparkles in the candlelight.

Swags of thick satin ribbon give a Victorian-style treatment to a traditional fire surround (make sure the ribbon trails hang well clear of the flames!).

WREATHS MAKE excellent wall decorations. Add extra sparkle by wrapping ribbon around the wreath and fixing a fake flower in place when you tie the ribbon at the base of the wreath.

A cream rosette completes the look.

Imitation snowberries add a frosty touch.

Wide, white ribbon helps dress the creation.

THIN TAPER-STYLE candles make a great display with little effort, especially when massed together.

Embed the tapers in sand and splay them out for effect – this will also help prevent them from melting each other's wax.

A vintage-style tin bucket makes an attractive and unusual container.

Tie a bow of pretty ribbon around the bucket as a finishing touch.

CANDLES AND DECORATIONS

Transform plain-glass night-light holders in an instant with silver star stickers. Line several in a row on a mantelpiece or table for maximum effect.

Use mirrors to reflect candlelight by placing small circular mirrors or simple mirrored tiles beneath your candle holders.

Create an eye-catching centrepiece for a table; this wide, flat-bottomed bowl is perfect for a modern arrangement of leaves, flowers and pillar candles.

Create a winter decoration that's bursting with contrasting textures by filling a bowl with knobbly fir cones and smooth glass baubles in frosty tones.

Suspend metal lanterns by ribbon or string from the ceiling to provide a magical light to dine by when the evenings start to draw in.

Bring the seaside indoors. Line three traditional glass hurricane lanterns with a layer of sand, dot with tiny shells, then place a chunky church candle inside.

A thick pillar candle placed inside a glass lantern is always a sophisticated choice. Glass pebbles and decorations around the candle base add sparkle.

For an adult take on Hallowe'en pumpkins, hollow out a squash and cut out small circular holes in the sides. Light the squash from within with a night light.

INDEX

index

ACKNOWLEDGEMENTS

Executive Editor Katy Denny
Senior Editor Charlotte Macey
Executive Art Editor Penny Stock
Designer one2six
Senior Production Controller Amanda Mackie

Photography

IPC+ Syndication/Essentials/Nick Pope 241 top left, 248, 249 top, 250 top left, 251 bottom left; /Ideal Home/Graeme Ainscough 71, 109, 111 top left, 121; /Susie Bell 38, 186, 235 top right; /Dominic Blackmore 41 top left, 116; /David Brittain 1 left, 16, 28, 31, 32, 37, 51 top left, 58, 59 top, 59 bottom, 64-65, 66, 72, 73, 77, 79, 83 bottom left, 93 top right, 94 top, 94 bottom, 95, 127 bottom right, 131, 133, 140 bottom left, 145, 146 top right, 170, 176, 180, 187, 212, 215, 224 top right, 224 bottom left, 224 bottom right, 225 top left, 226 top left, 228 top left, 229 top right, 229 bottom right, 232 bottom left, 233 bottom left; /Tamra Cave 104; /Darren Chung 125 top left; /Penny Cottee 82 top right; /Nikki Crisp 6; /Brent Darby 118 top left; /Dan Duchars 5 centre right, 12, 13, 17, 18, 19, 22, 29 top, 33, 35, 44, 46 top right, 51 centre right, 52, 53 top, 53 bottom, 80, 87 bottom, 91, 110, 112, 113, 118 bottom right, 123, 130 centre right, 132 top, 136, 137, 139, 141 bottom left, 147 top, 168-169, 176, 181, 183, 214, 216, 217, 218 top left, 219, 221 top right, 221 bottom left, 223 bottom right, 227 top left, 228 bottom right, 230 top left, 230 bottom left, 233 top right, 235 top left, 237 centre, 238, 239 top right, 239 bottom right, 240, 241 centre right, 241 bottom left, 245 top, 245 bottom, 247 top left, 250 top right, 250 bottom left, 251 top right; /David Garcia 195; /Stewart Grant 111 bottom right; /Tim Imrie 130 bottom left, 189; /Holly Joliffe 25, 47, 93 bottom left, 98 top, 98 bottom, 99, 147 bottom left, 178 centre right, 178 bottom left, 231 bottom right, 232 top left, 237 top left, 243 centre right, 246 top left; /Gareth Morgans 23; /Myles New 246 top right; /David Parmiter 120 top right, 225 bottom right; /Roland Paschhoff 188; /Bridget Peirson 67, 119 top right; /Spike Powell 5 top right, 14, 81, 117 bottom right, 175, 199, 210-211, 235 bottom left, 235

bottom right; /Mark Scott 8-9, 11, 30, 40, 41 bottom right, 43 bottom, 46 bottom left, 49 top right, 83 top right, 115, 122 top right, 122 bottom left, 125 bottom right, 126, 127 top left, 143, 173, 191, 201, 226 bottom left, 227 top right, 227 bottom left, 237 top right, 237 bottom left, 242, 244, 246

bottom left, 247 bottom left, 247 bottom right; /Simon Whitmore 2, 4, 10, 15, 20, 21, 24, 26, 27, 34, 36 top right, 36 bottom left, 43 top, 45, 48, 49 bottom left, 51 top right, 51 centre left, 51 bottom left, 51 bottom right, 54, 55 top, 55 bottom, 56, 57 top, 57 bottom, 60, 61 top, 61 bottom, 62, 63 top, 63 bottom, 68, 69, 76, 78, 84, 88, 90, 93 top left, 93 centre left, 93 centre right, 93 bottom right, 96 top, 96 bottom, 97, 100 top, 100 bottom, 101, 102 top, 102 bottom, 103, 106, 107 top left, 108, 114 top right, 114 bottom left, 117 top left, 119 bottom right, 124, 128 top left, 128 bottom right, 129, 134 top, 134 bottom, 135, 140 top right, 141 top right, 142 top right, 142 bottom left, 142 bottom right, 144, 146 bottom left, 171, 172, 174, 177, 179, 182, 213 bottom right, 218 bottom right, 220, 222, 224 top left, 225 top right, 225 bottom left, 226 top right, 226 bottom right, 230 top right, 230 bottom right, 231 top left, 232 top left, 233 top left, 233 bottom right, 234 top left, 234 top right, 234 bottom left, 234 bottom right, 251 bottom right; /Tim Winter 5 bottom right, 29 bottom, 39, 70, 85, 87 top, 132 bottom, 138, 190, 213 top left, 227 bottom right, 228 top right, 228 bottom left, 229 top left, 229 bottom left, 231 top right, 231 bottom left, 232 top right, 232 bottom right, 237 centre left, 237 bottom right, 243 top left, 243 bottom left, 246 bottom right, 247 top right, 250 bottom right, 251 top left; /Viv Yeo 120 bottom left; /Tim Young 89, 107 bottom right; /Paul Zammit 82 bottom left

acknowledgements